CORONA

SELECTED POEMS OF

PAUL CELAN

Translated by

Susan H. Gillespie

Station Hill

of Barrytown

Published by Station Hill of Barrytown, the publishing project of the Institute for Publishing Arts, Inc., 120 Station Hill Road, Barrytown, NY 12507, New York, a not-for-profit, tax-exempt organization [501(c)(3)].

This publication is supported in part by grants from the New York State Council on the Arts, a state agency.

Online catalogue: www.stationhill.org   e-mail: publishers@stationhill.org

Interior and cover design by Susan Quasha
Cover photo of Paul Celan (Vienna, 1948) © Eric Celan

Library of Congress Cataloging-in-Publication Data

Celan, Paul.
  [Poems. English. Selections]
  Corona: Selected poems of Paul Celan / translated by Susan H. Gillespie.
    pages cm
  ISBN 978-1-58177-127-5
  I. Gillespie, Susan H., translator. II. Title.
  PT2605.E4A2 2013
  831'.914—dc23

                    2012046518

CONTENTS

PREFACE

Corona: in English, a halo, or aureole. In German (and Italian), also: a fermata, the indeterminate "hold" of a musical note or rest. Both visual and aural, the corona radiates or resonates out from discrete experiences, including language and music. It echoes. Despite its stable appearance, it is always oscillating, as it hovers between memory and expectation. Within this charmed circle, writer, reader, and translator listen and speak to each other. They engage in a conversation.

The translations in this volume are the result of such a conversation—a decades-long engagement with Paul Celan's writing, its coronas, and the voluminous literature that has grown up around them. [1]

The selection includes poems written in German from all of Celan's periods and genres. Without ignoring the poet's justly heralded work of memory and memorialization, they seek to open a space for new appreciation of his love poems, as well as his poems on political events, painful reflections on his stays in mental hospitals, and quasi-burlesque verse. Well-known poems ("Tenebrae," "Psalm") stand next to early, Surrealist-influenced verse ("Chanson of a Lady in the Shadow"); poems on the Spanish civil war and the wars in Algeria and Vietnam ("Shibboleth," "In One," "To a Brother in Asia"); ironic ballads spiced with coded personal references ("Ballad of a Vagabond and Swindler," "La Contrescarpe," "Harbor"); poems that locate Celan's work in an intellectual landscape of other poets and historical figures and events ("In Memoriam Paul Éluard," "Zurich, 'The Stork,'" "Everything is otherwise," "Todtnauberg," "You lie"); and—last but not least—the miraculously compressed and probing poems that record Celan's ceaseless, philosophically informed, and dialogical inquiry into the play of language and meaning.

---

[1] For a further examination of the use of the image-concept "corona" in Celan, including its philosophical antecedents, see the Translator's Introduction.

With one exception, the order of the poems is the same as that in which they appeared in print, in the volumes *Poppy and Memory* (*Mohn und Gedächtnis*, 1952), *From Threshold to Threshold* (*Von Schwelle zu Schwelle*, 1955), *Speech-Grille* (*Sprachgitter*, 1959), *The No-one's Rose* (*Die Niemandsrose*, 1963), *Breathturn* (*Atemwende*, 1967), *Threadsuns* (*Fadensonnen*, 1968), *Darkened In* (*Eingedunkelt*, 1991), *Forced Light* (*Lichtzwang*, 1970), *Snowpart*, (*Schneepart*, 1971), and *Farmstead of Time* (*Zeitgehöft*, 1976). The exception is *Darkened In*, which was published twenty years after Celan's death. This volume contains poems that had appeared earlier in a collection of "abandoned works" of various authors (*Aus aufgegebenen Werken*, Suhrkamp, 1968), as well as a few poems that, after Celan's death, were found among a group of poems that Celan apparently prepared for publication under the title *Darkened In*. Although not published during Celan's lifetime, these poems ("The vacant center," "The glowing branding iron here," and "Don't be extinguished,") were included in the first edition of *Darkened In*, edited by Bertrand Badiou and Jean-Claude Rambach. The poems were written between February and May, 1966, when Celan was an inpatient at St. Anne's University Hospital, Paris, and was completing the final text of *Threadsuns*. The poems from *Darkened In* have been placed in chronological order before the other posthumous volumes.

Many resources are available nowadays to help us understand and mine the context of Celan's poems, including their sometimes coded and often overlapping references. Barbara Wiedemann's invaluable compilation of all the published and unpublished poems (*Paul Celan. Kommentierte Gesamtausgabe.* Suhrkamp, 2005) provides a concordance of sources for the life experiences and literary and other intellectual encounters that fed into Celan's writing consciousness. Very interesting is *La Bibliothèque philosophique: Catalogue raisonné des annotations*, compiled by Alexandra Richter, Patrik Alac, and Bertrand Badiou, with a preface by Jean-Pierre Lefebvre (Éditions rue d'Ulm, 2004), reproducing the marginal notes in Celan's extensive philosophical library. Of particular value, in the context of translation, is the volume *Fremde Nähe: Celan als Übersetzer* (*Foreign Nearness: Celan as Translator.* Deutsche Schillergesellschaft, 1997), from an exhibition by Axel Gellhaus and others on Celan's extremely varied, extensive, and mostly self-chosen work as a translator. The correspondence between Celan and his wife Gisèle Lestrange, with its extensive chronology; the still incomplete historical-critical edition of Celan's works; and the so-called Tübinger Edition, containing versions and materials related to Celan's poems and "Meridian" speech (all published by Suhrkamp), offer much additional food for thought. The Notes that follow the poems in this volume draw on these and other sources, with the intent to help interested readers identify references and situate the poems in their various possible contexts.

Translation, for me as for most translators, is an intensely inward and private act. Immersion in the text sets off reverberations that oscillate in and between the language of the original and the "new" language, intersecting in sometimes surprising ways and always heading somewhere else. I liken the effect both to Celan's image-concept of the corona and to the moving net that is woven by light as it passes through flowing water. The name for this phenomenon is "caustic." The poem at the end of this volume, "Water, Light, Darkness, Stone: In the Space of Translation with Paul Celan," is a product of this type of "caustic," as I see it tracing the moving, overlapping, and intersecting boundaries between Celan's language, my language, and two of our other languages, German and English.

This volume would never have come into being without the encouragement and assistance of many people. George Quasha and Susan Quasha, of Station Hill Press, and Robert Kelly deserve first place among those who have believed in this work and, over the years, encouraged me to share it publicly. Robert, together with Bruce McPherson, invited me to read in public for the first time. Franz Kempf and fellow translators Pierre Joris and Susan Bernofsky were generous in their praise and encouragement. Translations by Joris, Michael Hamburger, John Felstiner, Rosmarie Waldrop, and Ian Fairley, among others, showed that translation entails gains as well as losses. I am grateful to Willis Barnstone for his careful reading and thoughtful comments on the Celan translations, and I owe special thanks to Norman Manea and Stanley Moss for the incomparable opportunity to translate the correspondence between Paul Celan and Ilana Shmueli, including twenty-seven poems.[2] Shmueli, with

---

[2] *The Correspondence of Paul Celan & Ilana Shmueli,* translated by Susan H. Gillespie (Riverdale: Sheep Meadow Press, 2010).

her friend Barbara Schmutzler, offered invaluable insights into Celan and his work—Ilana's death in 2011 is a grave loss. I thank Leon Botstein, Lynn Holstein, and Lydia Goehr for their friendship and encouragement, and my daughters Jennifer Kapczynski and Amy Kapczynski for being a continuing inspiration. Peter Stern, Helen Drutt English, and Jim Ottaway, Jr., gave their unstinting admiration to the work and listened to my readings of many of the poems. Their generosity has helped make this publication possible. Thanks are due, finally, to Suhrkamp's Petra Hardt, in Berlin, and to Bertrand Badiou and Eric Celan, in Paris, for their permission to add these translations to the many already available.

✍

Coda: Celan's coronas are to be heard as well as seen. The translations in this volume, like Celan's German originals, will benefit by being read aloud.

Translator's Introduction

✍

The too-short life of Paul Celan (1920-1970) unfolded at the intersection of languages and countries, as he moved across their borders, torn and driven by the violence of their conflicts and the persecution he suffered as a Jew. His biography moves from Bukovina (at first part of Austro-Hungary, annexed by Romania and then by the Soviet Union—now Ukraine) to Bucharest, Vienna, and Paris, with frequent visits to Germany. Alongside the poetry (in German, with excursions into Romanian and French), and less than half a dozen remarkable prose pieces, Celan's oeuvre includes translations of forty-five authors from seven languages.[1] His poetry, as he repeatedly explained, was an attempt to make sense of all this, to find a direction, a way to live, in language.

The result is a poetry written in German and yet always written between languages, a poetry for which translation was and is a constitutive part of experience. Here, poetry is not what gets lost in translation, it is, itself, an act of translation—of experience and thought—into new language.

The poems in this selection have been translated, from Celan's German into my American English, over the course of three decades. During these years, my own life has frequently taken me across boundaries and borders, on my own

---

[1] Guillaume Apollinaire, Teodor Arghezi, Antonin Artaud, Charles Baudelaire, Alexander Blok, André Breton, Jean Cayrol, Aimé Césaire, René Char, Émil Cioran, Jean Daive, Robert Desnos, Emily Dickinson, John Donne, André Du Bouchet, Jacques Dupin, Paul Éluard, Robert Frost, Yvan Goll, Alfred Edward Housman, Vladimir Khlebnikov, Maurice Maeterlinck, Stéphane Mallarmé, Osip Mandelstam, Andrew Marvell, Vladimir Mayakovsky, Henri Michaux, Marianne Moore, Gellu Naum, Gérard de Nerval, Henri Pastoureau, Benjamin Péret, Ferdinand Pessoa, Pablo Picasso, Arthur Rimbaud, David Rokeah (Hebrew), William Shakespeare, Simenon, Konstantin Slutschevskiy, Jules Supervielle, Virgil Teodoresco, Giuseppe Ungaretti, Paul Valéry, Sergei Yesenin, Yevgeny Yevtushenko.

search for direction and meaning. Worked on not only at my own desk, but in airplanes or foreign places as well, the translations are intensely lived with.

The selection is my own. Some of the poems simply spoke to me more clearly or forcefully than others, or resonated in a way that I felt would work well in English. At the same time, I have attempted to make the selection at least somewhat representative. The reader for whom Paul Celan's poetry is a new discovery should be able to gain a broad sense of the course of his career as a writer. The individual poems are chronologically ordered, and I have gathered them under the titles of the volumes in which they appeared.

The earliest poems (*Poppy and Memory*) are from 1945-51, when Celan, still living in or recently departed from Bucharest, was affiliated with a group of French and Romanian Surrealists. I take this influence to be more important and lasting than it is sometimes considered to be. The Surrealists' revolutionary approach to language shaped Celan's tendency to forge contradictory, clashing impressions and memories into a single verbal image (often a new compound word), and his willing participation in a "linguistic unconscious" that connected him to other poets and their times.

Written from Paris, where Celan was making his living as a translator and teacher of German literature, the poems of Celan's mature middle period (*From Threshold to Threshold, Speech Grille, The No-one's Rose*) are incomparable in their compression and singularity. They include love poems—some of the most beautiful ones I know; meditations on language, especially poetic language and its capacity to remember and memorialize the past; and passionate questionings on the irresolvable problem of theodicy, of god's responsibility for evil. Several poems expressly address the experience of translating, both generally and in particular regard to his relationship to the Russian poet Osip Mandelstam, whose fate so closely resembled his own. We also find the first of his political poems, referring to the Spanish Civil War and expressing Celan's left-leaning background and orientation; he had been a Communist in his youth, and toward the end of his life he still loved to sing the old workers' songs. Also in this period, the first of the poems written in a rather different idiom appear—sharply ironic, balladesque, speaking in an assumed voice, and at the same time loaded with coded personal references.

The poems, taken as a whole, are invisibly interwoven in what Celan might have termed "constellations" of meaning, which extend beyond the individual text to create a harmonic architecture of echoes and references. We are present at the creation of a world, perhaps even a universe of meaning. To find one's way around and begin to identify the constellations takes some attentiveness on the part of the reader or listener. Asked about the best way to understand his poems, Celan's response was always the same: "Read them, and read them again." Reading them, and reading them again—out loud, if possible—one begins to hear the echoes that ricochet among them, creating a dense web of interconnections that hold the poems together, allowing them to speak back and forth to each other, as well as to us, their readers.

Toward the end of his life, from the beginning of 1963 until his suicide in April 1970, Celan's poems (*Breathturn*, *Threadsuns*, *Darkened In*, and the posthumously published *Forced Light*,[2] *Snowpart*, and *Farmstead of Time*) reflect, among other things, the agonized experience of his time spent in mental wards. During the final years, he lived alone, separated from his wife and son, and suffering the effects of medications that he felt were "healing him to pieces." Many of these later poems are written against loneliness and despair, seeking, in thought and experience, in philosophy (including Lao Tsu and other Chinese philosophers), and in a deepening engagement with Judaism, what he would have called "orientation," something to hold on to. This is not to say that these poems are not often gorgeously real in the spare language of their intensity. There are some happier ones, too, especially within the cycle written and dedicated to Ilana Shmueli, recently published by Sheep Meadow Press as part of the lovers' correspondence.[3]

Celan has been anthologized and canonized as a poet of the Holocaust—a word he himself never used. He preferred to speak of "what happened": an event, or catastrophic series of events, for which no adequate

---

[2] The volume *Forced Light* appeared in English as *Light-duress*, in Pierre Joris's prize-winning translation.

[3] *The Correspondence of Paul Celan & Ilana Shmueli*, translated by Susan H. Gillespie (Riverdale: Sheep Meadow Press, 2010).

single concept could exist. Celan disagreed with Theodor W. Adorno's dictum that "to write poems after Auschwitz is barbaric." From the beginning, Celan's own poetry was proof positive that it *was* possible (and the opposite of barbaric), that, on the contrary, it was necessary. Under pressure from Celan's friend Peter Szondi, among others, Adorno eventually recanted. No doubt, Celan's loss of both parents—especially of his mother, to whom he was particularly close—to the Nazis' extermination campaign and his experience of oppression and discrimination by both German and Russian totalitarianisms were defining experiences. So were the suicides of several friends of his youth, the cruelty and banality of a Socialist revolution that Celan originally welcomed, and the continuing anti-Semitism he experienced on his frequent trips to Germany, and not only there.

But there is so much more! I am drawn to his love poetry, its sidereal expansiveness on the one hand, its open (and sexy) sensuality on the other. The political poems include the disappointed elegy he wrote on the death of the Communist poet Paul Éluard, the poem he wrote after visiting the site in Berlin where Rosa Luxemburg and Karl Liebknecht were murdered on orders of the Social Democrats, and a gnomic comment on Berthold Brecht. And there are poems that can only be described as satirical, which I have mentioned above—longer poems in which Celan adopts the tone of a balladeer in verses that can be read as bitter, sardonic, and darkly funny.

A defining aspect of Celan's work, one that appears again and again in this selection, is his constant reflection on language itself and on the nature of poetic writing. The "metapoetic" thread runs through all the periods of Celan's writing, including the poems and prose works, and especially the "Meridian" speech that he gave in 1960 on the occasion of receiving Germany's most important literary prize. In the mid-1950s, Celan began working out a philosophically grounded poetics that was drawn from his own experience as a writer, from the 250 philosophical thinkers whose books peopled his library, and from his exposure to the poetry of Osip Mandelstam and the numerous modernist (mainly French) poets who were his associates and friends, and whom he translated. While "Meridian" gives the most fully developed exposition of Celan's poetological ideas, many of his poems—including some in this selection—also contain key insights.

As one of Celan's poems has it: *Wahr spricht, wer Schatten spricht*: He who speaks shadow speaks truly. We may hear, in the word "shadow," a reference to the dark hours of life, the remembrance of the dead, or the awareness of non-transparency in language. All are there. What matters is the—twice invoked—act of speaking. To *speak* truly—Celan's writing, circling in upon itself, is a single attempt, in seeking orientation, to write about life in all of its fullness, both good and evil, and at the same time to find a direction forward, to speak *truly*. Indeed, speaking, to each other and to ourselves, is our only means of attempting to find truth—even *the* truth. As Celan knew, *the* truth, in principle, is unattainable for humans, but we might just possibly, fleetingly, catch a glimpse of it, as Celan said in "Meridian," "in the light of Utopia."

(I think here, too, of the light Celan once reported seeing under a doorway, during a visit to his aunt Berta Antschel in London, which he took for a presence of the divine. This light—also *"Ziv*, that light," in a reference to Jewish tradition that Celan invoked in his poem to Sachs, "Zurich, 'The Stork'"—shines only intermittently and indirectly.)

One of the questions every reader or translator of poems has to wrestle with is how much one should know about their background in order to come up with the most productive and responsibly creative interpretation. The short answer—particularly important for the translator—is *everything*: as much as possible. Where it is possible to know, in detail, what the poet was doing, reading, and thinking around the time of the genesis of a particular poem, I want to know it. At the same time, it seems important to avoid over-emphasizing the personal experience. The poems themselves—in principle—are open to different interpretations. In translating them, therefore, while I attempt to learn as much as I can about their genesis, one of my main objectives is to preserve not only the imagery and the rhetorical and somatic quality of the language, but also its openness, its ambiguities. Where it seemed appropriate I have provided a note, relegated to the Notes on the Poems at the back of the book, which contain information to help readers place a specific reference.

In revising his poems, Celan himself sometimes blurred their references to people and events. What he referred to as the poems' "opacity" also had a broader meaning. "Opacity" meant avoiding allegorical or symbolic references as much as overly personal ones. It meant refusing to engage in a poeticizing or distancing view of the world that would abstract from what he once, in an interview, called his "soul realism." Celan is insistent, in his writing, on reflecting and embodying lived experience. Lived experience itself is contradictory, paradoxical, and difficult enough to grasp.

To translate: to carry across. Celan's most emblematic poem about poetic creation—a poem I hold to be of central importance for understanding his work and poetics—contains the word *übersetzen*, "to translate," as part of a parable of carrying across. It is a truncated parable open to more than one meaning.

From Darkness to Darkness

You opened your eyes—I see my darkness live.
I see down to the bottom;
there too it's mine and lives.

Can this cross over? And thereby awaken?
Whose light follows at my heels
that a ferryman appeared?

Here is the poem in German:

Von Dunkel zu Dunkel

Du schlugst die Augen auf—ich seh mein Dunkel leben.
Ich seh ihm auf den Grund:
auch da ists mein und lebt.

Setzt solches über? Und erwacht dabei?
Wes Licht folgt auf dem Fuss mir,
dass sich ein Ferge fand?

A love poem? A poem about language? We see the poet in a small craft on a dark sea. It is a rather traditional image, even if the boat is present only by implication, at the close of the poem. The sea is deep, a black pond in the eyes of his beloved. The poet, with the help of a mysterious ferryman, crosses over, or asks about the possibility of crossing over. The German word that I have translated as "cross over" is *übersetzen:* to translate. Literally: does this translate? In a well-known aperçu by Martin Heidegger, with which Celan was familiar, the philosopher noted that *über-setz'-en,* as it is normally pronounced, with the accent on the second syllable, means "translate"; while with the accent on the first syllable, *über'-setz-en,* it means to ferry across or be ferried across. Celan exploits this ambiguity. Attempting to be open to both, and to stick close to Celan's questioning rhythm and rising tone, I have translated as "Can this cross over?"

The "this" in the poem, what it seems to be "about," initially, is darkness—or shall we rather assume two darknesses, the "darkness to darkness" of the title. One is the darkness of the poet, the other a darkness in the eyes of the beloved. The two darknesses may in fact resolve into a single darkness ("mine"): darkness + darkness = darkness. In this reading, the darkness that the poet sees reflected in the depth of a lover's gaze is his own darkness—separated now not by attribution, but by self-consciousness and the passage of time, in memory. And yet, it is almost impossible not to imagine that these two darknesses do not, on some level, belong to the lovers, that there isn't a place in the poem both for the darkness of the poet and for the darkness of the beloved (apart from the likely darkness of her eyes). Indeed, this is the question posed by the poem. Does the darkness cross over? Does it awaken? The poem does not answer this question, but the ferryman "appeared." There is the hope and possibility of crossing.

The darkness evoked in this poem reverberates through the "Meridian" speech. The poem, Celan writes there, has a darkness that, "if not congenital," is "attributed to it for the sake of an encounter, from a—perhaps self-created—distance or strangeness."[4] In this "for the sake of an encounter" we may see an affirmation of the interpersonal encounter that is at risk in the poem, for which the poem takes its risks.

The darkness attributed to the figures in the poem may cross over and awaken—at least we hope it will. It will cross over and awaken if the

---

[4] Here and elsewhere I cite Rosmarie Waldrop's fine translation of Celan's prose works, *Paul Celan: Collected Prose* (England: Carcanet, 1986).

ferryman does his job. The ferryman appears for the poet thanks to a mysterious light, the light of someone else ("whose"). This light—anomalous in a scene centered on a living, creative darkness that the poet hopes will cross over (and not be effaced by light), paradoxical in its task of awakening without driving off the darkness of sleep—does not lead the way, nor does it pour down from above, like the sun. Instead, it follows the movement of the poet, lights him and the scene from behind. If it throws a shadow, it is a shadow thrown forward, toward the other bank of the river, or toward the beloved at whom the poet still gazes. Backlit, it casts a silhouette in a mirror.[5] But at the same time, the light also follows the poet's movements, clings to the heel of his wandering foot. It seems to obey him, although it does this without his will. This shadow, into which the poet must step, is both self-created and completely dependent on a light from without. Its origin is interpersonal and alive—it follows, responds, clarifies, and reflects. It can be nothing but a form of mind, a shared consciousness. Only shared consciousness will allow the poet to embrace the present and an unknown future with the help of what he leaves behind, of the past.

The tenses in the poem are important. The simple past appears in two places: the beloved has opened her eyes, and a ferryman appeared. Thanks to the first of these two events, two things occur in the present: the poet sees and the darkness lives. And two questions are posed. In German, the questions are posed in the simple present: "Does this cross over, and thereby awaken?" I have translated somewhat differently, to emphasize the contingent nature of the crossing: "Can this cross over, and thereby awaken?" For the crossing remains uncertain, the destination ultimately unknown. In the future, if all goes well, there will be a crossing, and there will be an awakening. Such a thing as this (*Solches*) will arrive at its destination.

This *Solches*, this something, which I have translated inadequately as "this," adds a further dimension, a comparative element to the text. "Such

---

[5] Celan gave the title "Backlight (*Gegenlicht*)" to group of aphoristic prose pieces he published in a newspaper in 1949, and also to a cycle in the volume *Poppy and Memory*.

a thing as this" lifts the experience from the realm of the uniquely experienced to the level of the hypothetical. It also makes it generalizable. If the experience of this poem can cross over, then such crossings are repeatable, are possible as a type.

And the ferryman? The ferryman—we hope that he has come to appear for us as he appeared for Celan—is not the poet. This is important. Thinking of the ferryman as the poet, and the poem as his "freight," is a natural mistake, particularly given other references in Celan to the poem as a message in a bottle. Indeed it is a rather common topos. It recalls, as well, the mythical figure of Charon, the boatman who ferries souls across the river Styx, to Hades.

But in this poem the ferryman is *not* the poet. The ferryman can only be the poem itself. A living presence, the poem springs to life in the mysterious light of shared consciousness. In an interview in *Die Welt* that he gave in 1958, Celan spoke of the life of the poem in terms identical to those in "From Darkness to Darkness": "Poems sketch out life—they cast their shadow ahead of themselves: one must live after them. Life itself must pass through the poem."[6] If we think of Celan's poem as a love poem, we may imagine this shared consciousness, with Walter Benjamin, as the bearer of the "profane epiphany" of mutual love. In the German original, the word that I have translated as "appeared" is *sich fand*—a reflexive verb that in its most literal sense means "found himself" or "found itself." It's a judicious way of thinking about the mysterious, "found" quality of poetic inspiration. *Sich fand* can be also be translated as "was found," a variant that I seriously considered before opting, in the end, for "appeared" because of its suggestion of epiphany. If we think of the poem as being about poetry and/or translation, we may imagine it as the carrier and enabler of the sudden insight that flashes up when the words of the poet

---

[6] *Gedichte entwerfen Leben—sie werfen ihren Schatten voraus. Man muß ihnen nachleben. Das Leben selber muß durch das Gedicht hindurch.* Interview with Harry Neumann, *Die Welt*, 27 January 1958. Cited in Charlotte Ryland, *Paul Celan's Encounters with Surrealism. Trauma, Translation and Shared Poetic Space* (London: Legenda, 2010). Trans. by Charlotte Ryland.

are truly grasped, "made flesh" by his reader/translator. This interpretation is supported by Celan's use, in the opening line of the poem, of the verb *aufschlagen*, which is typically used of eyes—or of books.[7] If we think of it as a poem that, like quite a few in Celan, hallows the memory of the dead, we may imagine it, Charon-like, as responding to death's finality by transmuting our grief, for just a moment, into a living communion with the dead. In all of these possible interpretations—all of them justified— the poem arises out of darkness and out of the past and makes toward an uncertain, unknown future in which it hopes to be in the company of another. As Celan wrote in "Meridian," "The poem is lonely. It is lonely and *en route*. Its author stays with it." And:

> And are these paths [of poems] only detours, detours from you to you? But they are, among how many others, the paths on which language becomes voice. They are encounters, paths from a voice to a listening you, natural paths, outlines for existence perhaps. For projecting ourselves into the search for ourselves.... A kind of homecoming.

Everything Celan says here about poetry is also true of translation— translation as poetry, as a metaphor for the transfer of poetic meaning, its voicing, its practice.

Note: the author stays with the poem. This applies, as well, to poems in translation—the original author stays with them. In a letter from 1959, referring to his Mandelstam translations, Celan described the process of translation in a way that goes beyond the now conventional notion of an encounter with the text. Of course, the text is the starting point for any translation, and as Celan notes: "My translations bear witness to my continual effort to achieve philological precision." But there is something that extends beyond the text, that accompanies or radiates out from it. Celan continues: "Admittedly, the main thing for me, while remaining as close as possible to the text, was to translate the poetic in the poem, to reproduce

---

[7] Thanks to Madeleine Stratford for this observation.

the form, the timbre of the person who is speaking."[8] Here we see a double encounter: not only with the text, but with a trace presence, in the text, of the other poet, his "form" or "timbre," the quality of his voice.

For Celan, Mandelstam's "voice" resonated with his life history and the cruel times that inflicted suffering so tragically reminiscent of Celan's. The poet's voice also resonated in the physical shape of the poems, the choice of language and the poems' somatic form—rhythm, rhyme, assonance, and in general the gait and sound of their language. It is remarkable that Celan, who in his own work abandoned rhyme very early (except for occasional special effects) manages miraculously to recreate all of Mandelstam's poems in German rhymed stanzas.

In a radio program Celan wrote in 1960, he describes experiencing Mandelstam, in his poetry, as a conversation whose nature is "phenomenal":

> ...this phenomenon that emerges in the conversation has,
> like the person who perceived it with his language, its
> own time. Thus it comes toward you: in its very nearness
> distance is speaking, its own time speaks too; in the poem
> these—different—times interconnect, the hour speaks
> and the eon, the heartbeat and the cosmic clock....
> They talk to each other, draw closer together—they
> remain incommensurable. In this way in the poem, the
> movement and the tension emerge by which we recognize
> it: time always joins in, time *participates.* The poems of
> Osip Mandelstam stand in a temporal corona of this
> kind. Which is the source, even in the noun series, of
> that vibrato of the words, which (also) has semantic
> relevance.[9]

---

[8] Letter to Gleb Struve, January 29, 1959, cited in Leonard Ölschner, "'Anamnesis': Paul Celan's Translation of Poetry," In: *Translating Tradition: Paul Celan in France,* ed. by Benjamin Hollander (special double issue #8/9 of *ACTS: A Journal in New Writing*), p. 69. My translation.

[9] Published in *Paul Celan: Der Meridian. Endfassung—Vorstufen— Materialien,* ed. Bernhard Böschenstein and Heino Schmull (Frankfurt: Suhrkamp, 1999) 216. My translation.

The description of the poetic encounter as "phenomenal" and the mention of a "temporal corona" point to the philosopher Edmund Husserl, whose *Lectures on the Phenomenology of the Inner Consciousness of Time* Celan read in 1958. In the lectures, Husserl introduces the idea of the "temporal corona"—a term of art that Celan underlined in his copy of the *Lectures*, and that turns up more than once in his letters, poems, and other writings. The concept refers to Husserl's observation that experience never contains a purely present moment—if it did, if it were completely separate from what precedes and follows, it would be essentially meaningless. The neologism Husserl uses for this is *Zeithof*—a compound of *Zeit*, meaning "time," and *Hof*, meaning "courtyard" or "corona," for example the ring around the moon or the corona that becomes visible during a full eclipse of the sun or moon. Interestingly, German also recognizes the Italianate form "Corona" (sometimes written *Korona*), which—as in English—means "corona" in the senses given above, and also has a musical meaning—the fermata, or lengthening of a note or rest, represented by the symbol ⌒. Although the Germanic term *Hof* is purely spatial, this musical meaning of *Corona* in German seems to bleed over into Husserl's concept of the *Zeithof*, which relies for its definition on the example of musical melody: "The now-point again has a 'temporal corona' for consciousness, which occurs in a continuity of memory perceptions. The whole memory of the melody consists in a continuum of such temporal continuums, i.e. of continuums of perceptions of the type that have been described."[10]

"Corona" thus emerges as a rather significant notion—an image-concept that, as it oscillates between visual and aural sensory modes, different languages, and overlapping temporal domains, sets broad and flexible horizons for human experience. For Husserl as for Celan, the shifting languages and meanings enrich and complicate each other. In this way, the term "corona," in its various overlapping senses, both embodies and

---

[10] Edmund Husserl, Vorlesungen zur Phänomenologie des inneren Zeitbewußtseins (Lectures on the Phenomenology of the Inner Consciousness of Time), ed. Martin Heidegger (Tübingen: Max Niemeyer Verlag, 3rd edition, 2000), 396. My translation.

expresses the view that present perception is neither static nor disconnected from other perceptions, memories, and expectations or yearnings. Similarly, the apparently clear and present visual image, the precise poetic word is not unitary or closed in itself. It evokes something like an aura, a semi-visible, semi-audible, perhaps semi-conscious field of awareness that allows us to perceive the resonances with things and thoughts that are past or absent.

All this, as Celan repeatedly insists, has *semantic* meaning. The aural or visual corona, the fermata we sense within or behind the text are not just poetic devices, metaphors or allusions (despite the metaphorical quality of the terms themselves). In their multimodal, multilingual aspects they are real bearers of meaning. *They participate.* And the *way* they participate is by allowing resonances to unfold and become present to mind. The visual corona allows us to see peripheral light that is otherwise outshone by the brilliance of the sun or moon. The aural corona or fermata allows us to hear harmonic resonances that might otherwise be missed or drowned out. The temporal corona allows us to ascribe meaning to life experience, including the life and voice of the poem and its accompanying poet. In this way, the poem is free, as its readers and translators are also, and inescapably, free to assemble or intuit its meaning. We do this by drawing on the experiences and other phenomena we have stored up in our linguistic and perceptual unconscious.

The role of the corona or fermata as the opening of a space for the perception of resonances is, I think, related to the significance of silence in Celan—a silence that is open and resonant. To quote again from the radio program:

> It is this tension between the times, one's own and that
> of the other, that lends the poem by Mandelstam that
> painfully mute vibrato by which we recognize it. (This
> vibrato is everywhere: in the intervals between the words
> and the stanzas, in the "coronas" in which the rhymes and
> assonances stand, in the punctuation. All that has *semantic*
> relevance.) The things draw close to each other, but in this

very adjacency the question also arises: from where, and to where—an "open" question that "has no end," that points to something open and available, vacant and free.

The vibrato of the human hand or voice, with its trembling ambiguity and ultimate incommensurability, is inseparable from both its unique personal time and its historical times. It speaks from the singularity of a mortal and unrepeatable human life—what Celan once beautifully called its "angle of inclination" (*Neigungswinkel*). And yet, although incommensurable, the voice is not meaningless, nor does its ambiguity ultimately render translation impossible. On the contrary, it is precisely the persistence of the somatic, real-life timbre of the voice, the vibrato of a memory that is inseparable from its anticipated or longed-for future—that translation aims for. The *sound and shape* of physical, spoken language—which can also, of course, be its mental representation as heard while reading a text—are essential bearers of meaning.

CORONA

DIE HAND VOLLER STUNDEN, so kamst du zu mir—ich sprach:
Dein Haar ist nicht braun.
So hobst du es leicht auf die Waage des Leids, da war es schwerer als ich...

Sie kommen auf Schiffen zu dir und laden es auf, sie bieten es feil
                                auf den Märkten der Lust—
Du lächelst zu mir aus der Tiefe, ich weine zu dir aus der Schale, die
                                      leicht bleibt.
Ich weine: Dein Haar ist nicht braun, sie bieten das Wasser der See,
                          und du gibst ihnen Locken...
Du flüsterst: Sie füllen die Welt schon mit mir, und ich bleib dir
                         ein Hohlweg im Herzen!
Du sagst: Leg das Blattwerk der Jahre zu dir—es ist Zeit, daß du
                      kommst und mich küssest!

Das Blattwerk der Jahre ist braun, dein Haar ist es nicht.

YOUR HAND FULL OF HOURS, so you came to me—I spoke:
Your hair is not brown.
You lifted it light on the suffering-scale, and lo, it was heavier than I...

They come on ships, they pile it high, they are huckstering it in the
markets of lust—
You smile at me from the depths, I cry to you from the scale, which stays
light.
I cry: your hair is not brown, they offer sea water; you give them locks...
You whisper: they're filling the whole world with me, and I'm still a hollow
worn in your heart!
You say: Make the leafwork of years your own—it is time for you to come
kiss me!

The leafwork of the years is brown, your hair is not.

CHANSON EINER DAME IM SCHATTEN

Wenn die Schweigsame kommt und die Tulpen köpft:
Wer gewinnt?
           Wer verliert?
                      Wer tritt an das Fenster?
Wer nennt ihren Namen zuerst?

Es ist einer, der trägt mein Haar.
Er trägts wie man Tote trägt auf den Händen.
Er trägts wie der Himmel mein Haar trug im Jahr, da ich liebte.
Er trägt es aus Eitelkeit so.

Der gewinnt.
           Der verliert nicht.
                      Der tritt nicht ans Fenster.
Der nennt ihren Namen nicht.

Es ist einer, der hat meine Augen.
Er hat sie, seit Tore sich schließen.
Er trägt sie am Finger wie Ringe.
Er trägt sie wie Scherben von Lust und Saphir:
er war schon mein Bruder im Herbst;
er zählt schon die Tage und Nächte.

Der gewinnt.
           Der verliert nicht.
                      Der tritt nicht ans Fenster.
Der nennt ihren Namen zuletzt.

Es is einer, der hat, was ich sagte.
Er trägts unterm Arm wie ein Bündel.
Er trägts wie die Uhr ihre schlechteste Stunde.
Er trägt es von Schwelle zu Schwelle, er wirft es nicht fort.

PAUL CELAN

Chanson of a Lady in the Shadows

When the silent lady comes and beheads the tulips:
Who wins?
                    Who loses?
                                        Who goes to the window?
Who says her name first?

There is someone, he wears my hair.
He wears it the way we bear the dead, on his hands.
He wears it the way heaven wore my hair in the year when I loved.
He wears it that way out of vanity.

He wins.
                    Does not lose.
                                        Does not go to the window.
He does not say her name.

There is someone who has my eyes.
He has had them since gates have been closing.
He wears them like rings on his finger.
He wears them like splinters of lust and sapphire:
in the autumn, already, he was my brother;
he was already counting the days and nights.

He wins.
                    Does not lose.
                                        Does not go to the window.
He is the last one to say her name.

There is someone, he has what I said.
He carries it under his arm, like a bundle.
He bears it the way the clock bears its worst hour.
He bears it from threshold to threshold, does not cast it out.

Der gewinnt nicht.

   Der verliert.

      Der tritt an das Fenster.

Der nennt ihren Namen zuerst.

Der wird mit den Tulpen geköpft.

He does not win.
        He loses.
                He goes to the window.
He is the first to say her name.

He is beheaded with the tulips.

Corona

Aus der Hand frißt der Herbst mir sein Blatt: wir sind Freunde.
Wir schälen die Zeit aus den Nüssen und lehren sie gehn:
die Zeit kehrt zurück in die Schale.

Im Spiegel ist Sonntag,
im Traum wird geschlafen,
der Mund redet wahr.

Mein Aug steigt hinab zum Geschlecht der Geliebten:
wir sehen uns an,
wir sagen uns Dunkles,
wir lieben einander wie Mohn und Gedächtnis,
wir schlafen wie Wein in den Muscheln,
wir das Meer im Blutstrahl des Mondes.

Wir stehen umschlungen im Fenster, sie sehen uns zu von der Straße:
Es ist Zeit, daß man weiß!
Es ist Zeit, daß der Stein sich zu blühen bequemt,
daß der Unrast ein Herz schlägt.
Es ist Zeit, daß es Zeit wird.

Es ist Zeit.

Corona

From my hand autumn nibbles its leaf: we are friends.
We shell time from the nuts and teach it to walk:
time returns to the shell.

In the mirror is Sunday,
the dream enfolds sleeping,
the mouth speaks true.

My eye looks down to the sex of my lover:
we gaze at each other,
we speak of dark things,
we love each other like poppy and memory,
we sleep like wine in the clamshells,
like the sea in the moon's bloody ray.

We stand and embrace at the window, they watch us from the street:
It is time that they knew!
It is time that the stone decided to bloom,
that haste turned a heartwheel.
It is time to be time.

It is time.

KRISTALL

Nicht an meinen Lippen suche deinen Mund,
nicht vorm Tor den Fremdling,
nicht im Aug die Träne.

Sieben Nächte höher wandert Rot zu Rot,
sieben Herzen tiefer pocht die Hand ans Tor,
sieben Rosen später rauscht der Brunnen.

CRYSTAL

Not on my lips seek your mouth,
not at the gate the stranger,
not in the eye the tear.

Seven nights above, red and red converge,
seven hearts more deeply, the hand beats on the gate,
seven roses later the wellspring rushes.

AUF HOHER SEE

Paris, das Schifflein, liegt im Glas vor Anker:
so halt ich mit dir Tafel, trink dir zu.
Ich trink so lang, bis dir mein Herz erdunkelt,
so lange, bis Paris auf seiner Träne schwimmt,
so lange, bis es Kurs nimmt auf den fernen Schleier,
der uns die Welt verhüllt, wo jedes Du ein Ast ist,
an dem ich hänge als ein Blatt, das schweigt und schwebt.

On the High Seas

Paris, a tiny ship, lies anchored in the bottle
and so with you I sit at table, lift my glass
and drink until my heart grows dark toward you,
and Paris is swimming on its tear,
until it lays its course for the distant veil
that shrouds the world from us, where every thou's a branch
and I hang as a leaf that, silent, floats.

LANDSCHAFT

Ihr hohen Pappeln—Menschen dieser Erde!
Ihr schwarzen Teiche Glücks—ihr spiegelt sie zu Tode!

Ich sah dich, Schwester, stehn in diesem Glanze.

LANDSCAPE

You tall poplars—people of this earth!
You black ponds of bliss—you mirror them to death!

I saw you, sister, standing in this brilliance.

Ich hörte sagen

Ich hörte sagen, es sei
im Wasser ein Stein und ein Kreis
und über dem Wasser ein Wort,
das den Kreis um den Stein legt.

Ich sah meine Pappel hinabgehn zum Wasser,
ich sah, wie ihr Arm hinuntergriff in die Tiefe,
ich sah ihre Wurzeln gen Himmel um Nacht flehn.

Ich eilt ihr nicht nach,
ich las nur vom Boden auf jene Krume,
die deines Auges Gestalt hat und Adel,
ich nahm dir die Kette der Sprüche vom Hals
und säumte mit ihr den Tisch, wo die Krume nun lag.

Und sah meine Pappel nicht mehr.

I Heard Someone Say

I heard someone say there exists
in the water a stone and a ring
and over the water a word
that lays the ring over the stone.

I saw my poplar go down to the water,
I saw how her arm reached down to the deep,
saw her roots pleading upward toward heaven for night.

I did not hurry after her,
I only picked up from the earth that crumb
that has the shape and loft of your eyes,
I took from your throat the chain of remarks,
which I laid round the table on which the crumb lay.

And saw my poplar no more.

Von Dunkel zu Dunkel

Du schlugst die Augen auf—ich seh mein Dunkel leben.
Ich seh ihm auf den Grund:
auch da ists mein und lebt.

Setzt solches über? Und erwacht dabei?
Wes Licht folgt auf dem Fuß mir,
daß sich ein Ferge fand?

From Darkness to Darkness

You opened your eyes—I see my darkness live.
I see down to the bottom:
there too it's mine and lives.

Can this cross over? And thereby awaken?
Whose light follows at my heels
that a ferryman appeared?

STILLEBEN

Kerze bei Kerze, Schimmer bei Schimmer, Schein bei Schein.

Und dies hier, darunter: ein Aug,
ungepaart und geschlossen,
das Späte bewimpernd, das anbrach,
ohne der Abend zu sein.

Davor das Fremde, des Gast du hier bist:
die lichtlose Distel,
mit der das Dunkel die Seinen bedenkt,
aus der Ferne,
um unvergessen zu bleiben.

Und dies noch, verschollen im Tauben:
der Mund,
versteint und verbissen in Steine,
angerufen vom Meer,
das sein Eis die Jahre hinanwälzt.

Still Life

Candle by candle, shimmer by shimmer, shine by shine.

And this here, beneath it: an eye,
unpaired and shut,
lashing the lateness that dawned
without being the evening.

Before it the strangeness whose guest you are here:
the lightless thistle
with which the darkness recalls its own,
from afar,
in order to be unforgotten.

And this, too, buried in numbness:
the mouth,
turned stone and hard-bitten on stones,
called by the sea,
which churns its ice unto the years.

NÄCHTLICH GESCHÜRZT

Für Hannah und Hermann Lenz

Nächtlich geschürzt
die Lippen der Blumen,
gekreuzt und verschränkt
die Schäfte der Fichten,
ergraut das Moos, erschüttert der Stein,
erwacht zum unendlichen Fluge
die Dohlen über dem Gletscher:

dies ist die Gegend, wo
rasten, die wir ereilt:

sie werden die Stunde nicht nennen,
die Flocken nicht zählen,
den Wassern nicht folgen ans Wehr.

Sie stehen getrennt in der Welt,
ein jeglicher bei seiner Nacht,
ein jeglicher bei seinem Tode,
unwirsch, barhaupt, bereift
von Nahem und Fernem.

Sie tragen die Schuld ab, die ihren Ursprung beseelte,
sie tragen sie ab an ein Wort,
das zu Unrecht besteht, wie der Sommer.

Ein Wort—du weißt:
eine Leiche.

Laiß uns sie waschen,
laß uns sie kämmen,

Pursed for the Night

For Hannah and Hermann Lenz

Pursed for the night
the lips of the flowers
crossed and opposed
the shafts of the pinetrees,
grayed the moss, shattered the stone,
awakened to endless flight
the jackdaws over the glacier:

this is the place where
they rest whom we overtook:

they will not name the hour,
not count the flakes,
not follow the waters to the weir.

They stand apart in the world,
each one next to his night,
each one next to his death,
crude, bareheaded, rimed
with frost far and near.

They are paying down the debt that inspired their beginning,
they are paying it to a word
that has no right to exist, like the summer.

A word—you know:
a corpse.

Let us now wash it,
let us now comb it,

---

laß uns ihr Aug
himmelwärts wenden.

let us now turn its eye
heavenward.

Welchen der Steine du hebst

Welchen der Steine du hebst—
du entblößt,
die des Schutzes der Steine bedürfen:
nackt,
erneuern sie nun die Verflechtung.

Welchen der Bäume du fällst—
du zimmerst
die Bettstatt, darauf
die Seelen sich abermals stauen,
als schütterte nicht
auch dieser
Äon.

Welches der Worte du sprichst—
du dankst
dem Verderben.

Whichever Stone You Pick Up

Whichever stone you pick up—
you strip bare
those things in need of the stones' protection:
naked, now
they replait the lichens.

Whichever tree you fell—
you frame
the bed on which
the souls pile up again
as if this eon
were not
also quaking.

Whichever word you speak—
you owe thanks
to destruction.

In Memoriam Paul Éluard

Lege dem Toten die Worte ins Grab,
die er sprach um zu leben.
Bette sein Haupt zwischen sie,
laß ihn fühlen
die Zungen der Sehnsucht,
die Zangen.

Leg auf die Lider des Toten das Wort,
das er jenem verweigert,
der du zu ihm sagte,
das Wort,
an dem das Blut seines Herzens vorbeisprang,
als eine Hand, so nackt wie die seine,
jenen, der du zu ihm sagte,
in die Bäume der Zukunft knüpfte.

Leg ihm dies Wort auf die Lider:
vielleicht
tritt in sein Aug, das noch blau ist,
eine zweite, fremdere Bläue,
und jener, der du zu ihm sagte,
träumt mit ihm: Wir.

In Memoriam Paul Éluard

Lay the words in the grave of the dead man
that he spoke in order to live.
Lay his head among them,
let him feel
the tongues of longing,
the tongs.

Lay the word on the lids of the dead man
that he denied to the one
who said "thou" to him,
the word
that leapt past his heart's blood,
as a hand as naked as his is
strung the one who said "thou" to him
up on the trees of the future.

Lay this word on his eyelids:
perhaps
into his eye, the still blue one,
will come a second, stranger blue,
and the one who said "thou" to him
will dream with him: We.

SCHIBBOLETH

Mitsamt meinen Steinen,
den großgeweinten
hinter den Gittern,

schleiften sie mich
in die Mitte des Marktes,
dorthin,
wo die Fahne sich aufrollt, der ich
keinerlei Eid schwor.

Flöte,
Doppelflöte der Nacht:
denke der dunklen
Zwillingsröte
in Wien und Madrid.

Setz deine Fahne auf Halbmast,
Erinnrung.
Auf Halbmast
für heute und immer.

Herz:
gib dich auch hier zu erkennen,
hier, in der Mitte des Marktes.
Ruf's, das Schibboleth, hinaus
in die Fremde der Heimat:
Februar. No pasarán.

Einhorn:
du weißt um die Steine,
du weißt um die Wasser,
komm,

Shibboleth

With all my stones
wept large
behind the bars,

they dragged me
into the midst of the market
the place
where the flag is unfurled, to which
I have sworn no allegiance.

Flute,
double flute of the night:
recall the dark
twin red dawn in
Vienna and Madrid.

Fly your flag at half mast,
memory.
At half mast
for today and forever.

Heart:
make yourself known here too,
here in the midst of the market.
Shout the shibboleth out
in the strangeness of home:
February. No pasarán.

Unicorn:
you know of the stones,
you know of the waters,
come,

ich führ dich hinweg
zu den Stimmen
von Estremadura.

I will lead you away
to the voices
of Estremadura.

KENOTAPH

Streu deine Blumen, Fremdling, streu sie getrost:
du reichst sie den Tiefen hinunter,
den Gärten.

Der hier liegen sollte, er liegt
nirgends. Doch liegt die Welt neben ihm.
Die Welt, die ihr Auge aufschlug
vor mancherlei Flor.

Er aber hielts, da er manches erblickt,
mit den Blinden:
er ging und pflückte zuviel:
er pflückte den Duft—
und die's sahn, verziehn es ihm nicht.

Nun ging er und trank einen seltsamen Tropfen:
das Meer.
Die Fische—
stießen die Fische zu ihm?

CENOTAPH

Strew your flowers, stranger, feel free to strew them:
you are passing them down to the depths,
the gardens.

The one who should have lain here lies
nowhere. Yet the world lies beside him,
the world that opened its eye
to various wreaths.

But he, when he saw some things, went among
the blind:
he went and plucked too much:
he plucked the scent—
and they who saw it did not forgive him.

Now he went and imbibed a strange drink:
the sea.
The fish—
did the fish flock to join him?

UNTEN

Heimgeführt ins Vergessen
das Gast-Gespräch unsrer
langsamen Augen.

Heimgeführt Silbe um Silbe, verteilt
auf die tagblinden Würfel, nach denen
die spielende Hand greift, groß,
im Erwachen.

Und das Zuviel meiner Rede:
angelagert dem kleinen
Kristall in der Tracht deines Schweigens.

Below

Brought home to forgetfulness
the guest dialogue of
our languorous eyes.

Brought home syllable by syllable
scattered on the dayblind dice
that the playing hand reaches for, large,
on waking.

And the too much of my talk:
congealed round the small
crystal lattice of your silence.

TENEBRAE

Nah sind wir, Herr,
nahe und greifbar.

Gegriffen schon, Herr,
ineinander verkrallt, als wär
der Leib eines jeden von uns
dein Leib, Herr.

Bete, Herr,
bete zu uns,
wir sind nah.

Windschief gingen wir hin,
gingen wir hin, uns zu bücken
nach Mulde und Maar.

Zur Tränke gingen wir, Herr.

Es war Blut, es war,
was du vergossen, Herr.

Es glänzte.

Es warf uns dein Bild in die Augen, Herr.
Augen und Mund stehn so offen und leer, Herr.
Wir haben getrunken, Herr.
Das Blut und das Bild, das im Blut war, Herr.

Bete, Herr.
Wir sind nah.

Tenebrae

Near are we, Lord,
near enough to grasp.

Already grasped, Lord,
clawed into each other, as if
the body of each one of us
was your body, Lord.

Pray, Lord,
pray to us,
we are near.

Bent by the wind we set forth
we set forth, to bow down
to hollow and maar.

To the trough we went, Lord.

It was blood, it was,
that you sacrificed, Lord.

It glittered.

It made your image fly up in our eyes, Lord.
Eyes and mouth stand so open and empty, Lord.
We have drunk, Lord.
The blood and the image within it, Lord.

Pray, Lord.
We are near.

BLUME

Der Stein.
Der Stein in der Luft, dem ich folgte.
Dein Aug, so blind wie der Stein.

Wir waren
Hände,
wir schöpften die Finsternis leer, wir fanden
das Wort, das den Sommer heraufkam:
Blume.

Blume—ein Blindenwort.
Dein Aug und mein Aug:
sie sorgen
für Wasser.

Wachstum.
Herzwand um Herzwand
blättert hinzu.

Ein Wort noch, wie dies, und die Hämmer
schwingen im Freien.

FLOWER

The stone.
The stone in the air that I followed.
Your eye, as blind as the stone.

We were
hands,
we ladled the darkness empty, we found
the word that came up the summer:
flower.

Flower—a blindman's word.
Your eye and my eye:
they provide
for water.

Growth.
Heartwall and heartwall
petals here too.

One more word like this and the hammers
swing free.

SCHNEEBETT

Augen, weltblind, im Sterbegeklüft: Ich komm,
Hartwuchs im Herzen.
Ich komm.

Mondspiegel Steilwand. Hinab.
(Atemgeflecktes Geleucht. Strichweise Blut.
Wölkende Seele, noch einmal gestaltnah.
Zehnfingerschatten—verklammert.)

Augen weltblind,
Augen im Sterbegeklüft,
Augen Augen:

Das Schneebett unter uns beiden, das Schneebett.
Kristall um Kristall,
zeittief gegittert, wir fallen,
wir fallen und liegen und fallen.

Und fallen:
Wir waren. Wir sind.
Wir sind ein Fleisch mit der Nacht.
In den Gängen, den Gängen.

Snow Bed

Eyes, world-blind, in the dying-abyss: I come,
fibrous growth in my heart.
I come.

Moon-mirror precipice. Down.
(Breath-flecked effulgence. Traces of blood.
Clouding soul, once more shape-nearing.
Ten-finger-shadows—gripping.)

Eyes world-blind
Eyes in the dying-abyss,
Eyes eyes:

The snow bed under us both, the snow bed,
crystal and crystal,
time-deep latticed we fall,
we fall and we lie and we fall.

And fall:
We were. We are.
We are one flesh with the night.
In the veins, in the veins.

Es war Erde in ihnen, und
sie gruben.

Sie gruben und gruben, so ging
ihr Tag dahin, ihre Nacht. Und sie lobten nicht Gott,
der, so hörten sie, alles dies wollte,
der, so hörten sie, alles dies wußte.

Sie gruben und hörten nichts mehr;
sie wurden nicht weise, erfanden kein Lied,
erdachten sich keinerlei Sprache.
Sie gruben.

Es kam eine Stille, es kam auch ein Sturm,
es kamen die Meere alle.
Ich grabe, du gräbst, und es gräbt auch der Wurm,
und das Singende dort sagt: Sie graben.

O einer, o keiner, o niemand, o du:
Wohin gings, da's nirgendhin ging?
O du gräbst und ich grab, und ich grab mich dir zu,
und am Finger erwacht uns der Ring.

Paul Celan

THERE WAS EARTH IN THEM, and
they dug.

They dug and they dug, thus passed
their day, their night. And they did not praise god,
who, as they heard, wanted all this,
who, as they heard, knew of all this.

They dug and they heard nothing more;
they did not become wise, invented no song,
thought up no language at all.
They dug.

There came a stillness, there came a storm,
and all the seas came too.
I dig, you dig, and the worm digs too,
and what sings there says: they are digging.

O one, o none, o no-one, o thou:
Where was it going, the journey to nowhere?
O you dig and I dig, and I dig myself toward you,
on our finger awakens the ring.

BEI WEIN UND VERLORENHEIT, bei
beider Neige:

ich ritt durch den Schnee, hörst du,
ich ritt Gott in die Ferne—die Nähe, er sang,
es war
unser letzter Ritt über
die Menschen-Hürden.

Sie duckten sich, wenn
sie uns über sich hörten, sie
schrieben, sie
logen unser Gewieher
um in eine
ihrer bebilderten Sprachen.

WITH WINE AND FORLORNNESS, both
declining:

I rode through the snow, do you hear,
I rode god into the distance—the nearness, he sang,
it was
our last ride over
the human-race hurdles.

They ducked whenever
they heard us above them, they
wrote, they
lied our whinnying over
into one
of their picturing languages.

Zurich, Zum Storchen

Für Nelly Sachs

Vom Zuviel war die Rede, vom
Zuwenig. Von Du
und Aber-Du, von
der Trübung durch Helles, von
Jüdischem, von
deinem Gott.

Da-
von.
Am Tag einer Himmelfahrt, das
Münster stand drüben, es kam
mit einigem Gold übers Wasser.

Von deinem Gott war die Rede, ich sprach
gegen ihn, ich
ließ das Herz, das ich hatte,
hoffen:
auf
sein höchstes, umröcheltes, sein
haderndes Wort—

Dein Aug sah mir zu, sah hinweg,
dein Mund
sprach sich dem Aug zu, ich hörte:

Wir
wissen ja nicht, weißt du,
wir
wissen ja nicht,
was
gilt.

PAUL CELAN

Zurich, "The Stork"

For Nelly Sachs

Of the too much we talked, of
too little. Of thou
and once again thou, of
the light that makes murky, of
Jewish things, of
your god.

Of
that.
On an Ascension Day, the
cathedral stood over us, came
with aught gold across the water.

Of your god we talked, I spoke
against him, I
let the heart I had
hope:
for
his highest, death-rattled, his
querulous word—

Your eye looked at me, looked away,
your mouth
spoke toward the eye, I heard:

We
don't know, after all, you know,
we
don't know, after all,
what
holds true.

THE NO-ONE'S ROSE

SOVIEL GESTIRNE, die
man uns hinhält. Ich war,
als ich dich ansah—wann?—
draußen bei
den andern Welten.

O diese Wege, galaktisch,
o diese Stunde, die uns
die Nächte herüberwog in
die Last unsrer Namen. Es ist,
ich weiß es, nicht wahr,
daß wir lebten, es ging
blind nur ein Atem zwischen
Dort und Nicht-da und Zuweilen,
kometenhaft schwirrte ein Aug
auf Erloschenes zu, in den Schluchten,
da, wo's verglühte, stand
zitzenprächtig die Zeit,
an der schon empor- und hinab-
und hinwegwuchs, was
ist oder war oder sein wird—,

ich weiß,
ich weiß und du weißt, wir wußten,
wir wußten nicht, wir
waren ja da und nicht dort,
und zuweilen, wenn
nur das Nichts zwischen uns stand, fanden
wir ganz zueinander.

PAUL CELAN

SO MANY CONSTELLATIONS
are held out to us. I was,
when I gazed at you—when?—
outside in
the other worlds.

O these paths, galactic,
o this hour that weighed
the nights over toward us into
the burden of our naming. It is,
I know it, not true
that we loved, there was only
a breath that went blindly between
there and not here and at times;
an eye that, comet-like, whirred
toward something extinguished, in the chasms,
and there, where it burned out, stood time,
gorgeous-titted,
on which was already clambering up and down
and away what
is or was or will be—,

I know,
I know and you know, we knew,
we did not know, we
were, after all, here and not there,
and at times, when
there was only nothing between us, we found
all the way to each other.

DEIN
HINÜBERSEIN heute Nacht.
Mit Worten holt ich dich wieder, da bist du,
alles ist wahr und ein Warten
auf Wahres.

Es klettert die Bohne vor
unserm Fenster: denk
wer neben uns aufwächst und
ihr zusieht.

Gott, das lasen wir, ist
ein Teil und ein zweiter, zerstreuter:
im Tod
all der Gemähten
wächst er sich zu.

Dorthin
führt uns der Blick,
mit dieser
Hälfte
haben wir Umgang.

YOUR
SUDDEN ABSENCE tonight.
With words I retrieved you. Here you are,
everything is true and a waiting
for true things.

The beanstalk is climbing
outside our window: think
who is growing alongside us
watching it.

God, as we read, is
a part and a second, a scattered one:
in the death
of all those who were mown down
he grows toward himself.

That way
our gaze leads us,
with this
half
we have concourse.

ZU BEIDEN HÄNDEN, da
wo die Sterne mir wuchsen, fern
allen Himmeln, nah
allen Himmeln:
Wie
wacht es sich da! Wie
tut sich die Welt uns auf, mitten
durch uns!

Du bist,
wo dein Aug ist, du bist
oben, bist
unten, ich
finde hinaus.

O diese wandernde leere
gastliche Mitte. Getrennt,
fall ich dir zu, fällst
du mir zu, einander
entfallen, sehn wir
hindurch:

Das
Selbe
hat uns
verloren, das
Selbe
hat uns
vergessen, das
Selbe
hat uns— —

PAUL CELAN

ON BOTH HANDS, there
where the stars grew for me, far
from all heavens, near
to all heavens:
What
a watching is there! How
the world opens up for us, right
through us!

You are
where your eye is, you are
above, are
below, I
grope my way out.

O this wandering vacant
hospitable center. Separated,
I fall toward you, you
fall toward me, fallen away
from each other we
see through:

The
same-thing
has
lost us the
same-thing
has
forgotten us, the
same
has us— —

PSALM

Niemand knetet uns wieder aus Erde und Lehm,
niemand bespricht unsern Staub.
Niemand.

Gelobt seist du, Niemand.
Dir zulieb wollen
wir blühn.
Dir
entgegen.

Ein Nichts
waren wir, sind wir, werden
wir bleiben, blühend:
die Nichts-, die
Niemandsrose.

Mit
dem Griffel seelenhell,
dem Staubfaden himmelswüst,
der Krone rot
vom Purpurwort, das wir sangen
über, o über
dem Dorn.

PAUL CELAN

PSALM

No one kneads us again from earth and clay,
no one conjures our dust.
No one.

Praised be thou, No one.
For your sake,
we will bloom.
Toward
you.

We were
a nothing, are, and ever
shall be, blooming:
the nothing-, the
no-one's rose.

With
the pistil soul-bright,
the stamen heaven-ravaged,
the corolla red
from the purple word that we sang
over, o over
the thorn.

TÜBINGEN, JÄNNER

Zur Blindheit über-
redete Augen.
Ihre—"ein
Rätsel ist Rein-
entsprungenes"—, ihre
Erinnerung an
schwimmende Hölderlintürme, möwen-
umschwirrt.

Besuche ertrunkener Schreiner bei
diesen
tauchenden Worten:

Käme,
käme ein Mensch,
käme ein Mensch zur Welt, heute, mit
dem Lichtbart der
Patriarchen: er dürfte,
spräch er von dieser
Zeit, er
dürfte
nur lallen und lallen,
immer-, immer-
zuzu.

("Pallaksch. Pallaksch.")

Tübingen, January

Eyes talked into
blindness,
their "A
riddle is everything
pure in origin"—their
remembrance of
swimming Hölderlin towers, gull-
o'er-whirred.

Visits of drowned carpenters with
these
diving words:

If
If a man came
If a man came into the world, today, with
the light-beard of
the patriarchs: he would have to
if he spoke of this
time, he
would have to
just babble and babble,
on- and
onandon.

("Pallaksh. Pallaksh.")

CHYMISCH

Schweigen, wie Gold gekocht, in
verkohlten
Händen.

Große, graue,
wie alles Verlorene nahe
Schwestergestalt:

Alle die Namen, alle die mit-
verbrannten
Namen. Soviel
zu segnende Asche. Soviel
gewonnenes Land
über
den leichten, so leichten
Seelen-
ringen.

Große. Graue. Schlacken-
lose.

Du, damals.
Du mit der fahlen,
aufgebissenen Knospe.
Du in der Weinflut.

(Nicht wahr, auch uns
entließ diese Uhr?
Gut,
gut, wie dein Wort hier vorbeistarb.)

ALCHEMICAL

Silence, like gold smelted
in coal blackened
hands.

Great, gray,
like everything lost, near
sister shape:

All the names, all the
names
also burned. So much
ash to be blessed. So much
land reclaimed
over
the light, so light
soul
rings.

Great. Gray. Slag-
less one.

You, then.
You with the pale
bud bitten open.
You in the wine flood.

(Is it not so, we too
were released by this hour?
Good,
good, how your word died past here.)

Schweigen, wie Gold gekocht, in
verkohlten, verkohlten
Händen.
Finger, rauchdünn. Wie Kronen, Luftkronen
um— —

Große. Graue. Fährte-
lose.
König-
liche.

Silence, like gold smelted, in
coal blackened, coal blackened
hands.
Fingers, smoke-thin. Like crowns, crowns of air
holding— —

Great. Gray. Track-
less one.
Kingly
woman.

EINE GAUNER- UND GANOVENWEISE
GESUNGEN ZU PARIS EMPRÈS PONTOISE
VON PAUL CELAN
AUS CZERNOWITZ BEI SADAGORA

> *Manchmal nur, in dunkeln Zeiten,*
> Heinrich Heine, "An Edom"

Damals, als es noch Galgen gab,
da, nicht wahr, gab es
ein Oben.

Wo bleibt mein Bart, Wind, wo
mein Judenfleck, wo
mein Bart, den du raufst?

Krumm war der Weg, den ich ging,
krumm war er, ja,
denn, ja,
er war gerade.

Heia.

Krumm, so wird meine Nase.
Nase.

Und wir zogen auch nach *Friaul.*
Da hätten wir, da hätten wir.
Denn es blühte der Mandelbaum.
Mandelbaum, Bandelmaum.

Mandeltraum, Trandelmaum.
Und auch der Machandelbaum.
Chandelbaum.

Ballad of a Vagabond and Swindler
Sung in Paris emprès Pontoise
By Paul Celan
From Czernowitz by Sadagora

Sometimes, only, in dark times
Heinrich Heine, "To Edom"

Back then, when there were still gallows,
then, was there not, there was still
something on high.

Where is my beard, wind, where
my Jewish star, where
my beard, that you pull?

Crooked was the path that I took,
it was crooked, yes,
for, yes,
it was straight.

Heia.

Crooked, my nose grows crooked.
Nose.

And we were heading for *Friuli.*
There we would have, there we would have.
For the almond tree blossomed.
Almond tree, tralmondee.

Almond dream, dralmondeem.
And the juniper tree.
The tallow tree.

Heia.
Aum.

Envoi

Aber,
aber er bäumt sich, der Baum. Er,
auch er
steht gegen
die Pest.

Haia.
Om.

Envoi

But,
but it rears its limbs up, the tree. It,
it too
stands against
the plague.

FLIMMERBAUM

Ein Wort,
an das ich dich gerne verlor:
das Wort
Nimmer.

Es war,
und bisweilen wußtest auch du's,
es war
eine Freiheit.
Wir schwammen.

Weißt du noch, daß ich sang?
Mit dem Flimmerbaum sang ich, dem Steuer.
Wir schwammen.

Weißt du noch, daß du schwammst?
Offen lagst du mir vor,
lagst du mir, lagst
du mir vor
meiner vor-
springenden Seele.
Ich schwamm für uns beide. Ich schwamm nicht.
Der Flimmerbaum schwamm.

Schwamm er? Es war
ja ein Tümpel rings. Es war der unendliche Teich.
Schwarz und unendlich, so hing,
so hing er weltabwärts.

Weißt du noch, daß ich sang?

GLIMMER TREE

A word
to which I lost you gladly:
the word
nevermore.

There was
and at moments you knew it too,
there was
a freedom.
We were swimming.

Do you still remember that I sang?
Sang with the glimmer tree—rudder.
We were swimming.

Do you still remember that you swam?
You lay open before me,
lay
before me,
lay before my for-
ward projecting soul.
I swam for both of us. I did not swim.
The glimmer tree swam.

Did it swim? There was
a puddle around it. It was the endless pool.
Black and endless, it hung,
hung down the world.

Do you still remember that I sang?

Diese—
o diese Drift.

Nimmer. Weltabwärts. Ich sang nicht. Offen
lagst du mir vor
der fahrenden Seele.

This—
o this drift.

Nevermore. Down the world. I did not sing. You
lay open before my
sailing soul.

DIE HELLEN
STEINE gehn durch die Luft, die hell-
weißen, die Licht-
bringer.

Sie wollen
nicht niedergehen, nicht stürzen,
nicht treffen. Sie gehen
auf,
wie die geringen
Heckenrosen, so tun sie sich auf,
sie schweben
dir zu, du meine Leise,
du meine Wahre—:

ich seh dich, du pflückst sie mit meinen
neuen, meinen
Jedermannshänden, du tust sie
ins Abermals-Helle, das niemand
zu weinen braucht noch zu nennen.

THE BRIGHT
STONES pass through the air, the bright
white ones, the light
bringers.

They don't want
to set, or fall, or
strike. They open
up,
like the modest
hedge roses, that's how they open,
they float
toward you, my softspoken,
you my true one——:

I see you, you pluck them with my
new, my
everyman's hands, you place them
into the Once-again-bright, which no one
needs to cry over or name.

WAS GESCHAH? Der Stein trat aus dem Berge.
Wer erwachte? Du und ich.
Sprache, Sprache. Mit-Stern. Neben-Erde.
Ärmer. Offen. Heimatlich.

Wohin gings? Gen Unverklungen.
Mit dem Stein gings, mit uns zwein.
Herz und Herz. Zu schwer befunden.
Schwerer werden. Leichter sein.

WHAT OCCURRED? The stone issued from the mountain.
Who awakened? Thou and I.
Language, language. Co-star. Fellow earth.
Poorer. Open. Right at home.

Where was it going? Toward still resounding.
With the stone, went with us twain.
Heart and heart. Adjudged too heavy.
Become more heavy. Be more light.

In Eins

Dreizehnter Feber. Im Herzmund
erwachtes Schibboleth. Mit dir,
Peuple
de Paris. *No pasarán.*

Schäfchen zur Linken: er, Abadias,
der Greis aus Huesca, kam mit den Hunden
über das Feld, im Exil
stand weiß eine Wolke
menschlichen Adels, er sprach
uns das Wort in die Hand, das wir brauchten, es war
Hirten-Spanisch, darin,

im Eislicht des Kreuzers "Aurora":
die Bruderhand, winkend mit der
von den wortgroßen Augen
genommenen Binde—Petropolis, der
Unvergessenen Wanderstadt lag
auch dir toskanisch zu Herzen.

Friede den Hütten!

In One

Thirteenth of February. In the heart mouth
a shibboleth wakens. With you,
people
of Paris. *No pasarán.*

Lambs on the left: he, Abadias,
the old man from Huesca, came with the dogs
across the field, in exile
stood—white—a cloud
of human nobility, he breathed
into our hands the word we required, it was
shepherd Spanish, in it,

in the ice light of the battleship "Aurora":
the brother-hand, waving, with the
blindfold removed from the
eyes, huge with words—Petropolis, destination
of the unforgotten, you held it, too, like Tuscany,
in your heart.

Peace to the huts!

HINAUSGEKRÖNT,
hinausgespien in die Nacht.

Bei welchen
Sternen! Lauter
graugeschlagenes Herzhammersilber. Und
Berenikes Haupthaar, auch hier,—ich flocht,
ich zerflocht,
ich flechte, zerflechte.
Ich flechte.

Blauschlucht, in dich
treib ich das Gold. Auch mit ihm, dem
bei Huren und Dirnen vertanen,
komm ich und komm ich. Zu dir,
Geliebte.

Auch mit Fluch und Gebet. Auch mit jeder
der über mich hin-
schwirrenden Keulen: auch sie in eins
geschmolzen, auch sie
phallisch gebündelt zu dir,
Garbe-und-Wort.

Mit Namen, getränkt
von jedem Exil.
Mit Namen und Samen,
mit Namen, getaucht
in alle
Kelche, die vollstehn mit deinem
Königsblut, Mensch, —in alle
Kelche der großen
Ghetto-Rose, aus der

CROWNED OUT,
spit out into the night.

Among what
stars! Nothing but pure
gray-beaten hearthammer silver. And
Berenice's crown hair, here too,—I plaited
plaited apart,
I plait, plait apart,
I am plaiting.

Blue chasm, into you
I drive the gold. With it too, which has been
wasted with whores and loose women
I come and I come. To you,
beloved.

Also with curses and prayers. Also with each
of the clubs that fly whirring
above me: they too
smelted together, they too
phallicly bundled toward you
sheaf-and-word.

With names, drenched
in that exile,
with names and semen,
with names, drenched
in all the
chalices standing full of your
king's blood, humanity—in all the
chalices of the great
ghetto rose, from whence

---

du uns ansiehst, unsterblich von soviel
auf Morgenwegen gestorbenen Toden.

(Und wir sangen die Warschowjanka.
Mit verschilften Lippen, Petrarca.
In Tundra-Ohren, Petrarca.)

Und es steigt eine Erde herauf, die unsre,
diese.
Und wir schicken
keinen der Unsern hinunter
zu dir,
Babel.

you observe us, immortal from so many
dead, snatched away on their morning errands.

(And we sang the "Varsovienne."
With reed-covered lips, Petrarch.
To tundra ears, Petrarch.)

And an earth rises up, our earth,
this one.
And we will not send
even one of ours down
to you,
Babel.

La Contrescarpe

Brich dir die Atemmünze heraus
aus der Luft um dich und den Baum:

so
viel
wird gefordert von dem,
den die Hoffnung herauf- und herabkarrt
den Herzbuckelweg—so
viel

an der Kehre,
wo er dem Brotpfeil begegnet,
der den Wein seiner Nacht trank, den Wein
der Elends-, der Königs-
vigilie.

Kamen die Hände nicht mit, die wachten,
kam nicht das tief
in ihr Kelchaug gebettete Glück?
Kam nicht, bewimpert,
das menschlich tönende Märzrohr, das Licht gab,
damals, weithin?

Scherte die Brieftaube aus, war ihr Ring
zu entziffern? (All das
Gewölk um sie her—es war lesbar.) Litt es
der Schwarm? Und verstand,
und flog wie sie fortblieb?

Dachschiefer Helling, —auf Tauben-
kiel gelegt ist, was schwimmt. Durch die Schotten

Paul Celan

LA CONTRESCARPE

Break your breathcoin out
of the air that surrounds you and the tree:

this
much
is required of him
whom hope has dragged this way and that
on the heart-hump—this
much

at the turning,
where he meets bread's arrow
that drank the wine of his nights, the wine
of misery's, of the king's
vigil.

Didn't the hands come too, that kept watch,
the deeply embedded
joy in their eye chalice?
Did it not come, with lashes,
the human-voiced March reed that gave light,
once, shining far?

Was the carrier pigeon lost, could its ring
be deciphered? (All that
mistiness near her—it was legible.) Did the flock
endure it? And understood,
and flew on when she failed to return?

Slate roof slipway—on doves'
keel what swims. Through the tiles

---

blutet die Botschaft, Verjährtes
geht jung über Bord:

> Über Krakau
> bist du gekommen, am Anhalter
> Banhof
> floß deinen Blicken ein Rauch zu,
> der war schon von morgen. Unter
> Paulownien
> sahst du die Messer stehn, wieder,
> scharf von Entfernung. Es wurde
> getanzt. (Quatorze
> juillets. Et plus de neuf autres.)
> Überzwerch, Affenvers, Schrägmaul
> mimten Gelebtes. Der Herr
> trat, in ein Spruchband gehüllt,
> zu der Schar. Er knipste
> sich ein
> Souvenirchen. Der Selbst-
> auslöser, das warst
> du.

O diese Ver-
freundung. Doch wieder,
da, wo do hinmußt, der eine
genaue
Kristall.

bleeds the message, everything old
goes young overboard:

> Via Crakow
> you came, near the Anhalter
> Bahnhof
> smoke billowed toward you—
> it came from tomorrow. Under
> Paulownias
> you saw, raised again, the knives,
> sharp with distance. There was
> dancing. *(Quatorze*
> *Juillets. Et plus de neuf autres.)*
> Crosswise, ape rhymes, twisted mouth
> mimed life. The gentleman,
> wrapped in a slogan, joined
> the crowd. He shot
> himself
> a souvenir. The automatic shutter
> was
> you.

O this false
friending. Yet, once again,
there, where you must go, the one
precise
crystal.

Es ist Alles anders

Es ist Alles anders als du es dir denkst, als ich es mir denke,
die Fahne weht noch,
die kleinen Geheimnisse sind noch bei sich,
sie werfen noch Schatten, davon
lebst du, leb ich, leben wir.

Die Silbermünze auf deiner Zunge schmilzt,
sie schmeckt nach Morgen, nach Immer, ein Weg
nach Rußland steigt dir ins Herz,
die karelische Birke
hat
gewartet,
der Name Ossip kommt auf dich zu, du erzählst ihm,
was er schon weiß, er nimmt es, er nimmt es dir ab, mit Händen,
du löst ihm den Arm von der Schulter, den rechten, den linken,
du heftest die deinen an ihre Stelle, mit Händen, mit Fingern, mit Linien,

—was abriß, wächst wieder zusammen—
da hast du sie, da nimm sie dir, da hast du alle beide,
den Namen, den Namen, die Hand, die Hand,
da nimm sie dir zum Unterpfand,
er nimmt auch das, und du hast
wieder, was dein ist, was sein war,

Windmühlen

stoßen dir Luft in die Lunge, du ruderst
durch die Kanäle, Lagunen und Grachten,
bei Wortschein,
am Heck kein Warum, am Bug kein Wohin, ein Widderhorn hebt dich

---

PAUL CELAN

EVERYTHING IS OTHERWISE

Everything is otherwise than you think, than I think,
the banner still waves,
the little secrets still keep to themselves,
they still cast shadows, from them
you live, I live, we live.

The silver coin on your tongue melts,
it smells of morning, of Always, a path
to Russia mounts to your heart,
the Karelian birch tree
has
waited,
the name Osip comes toward you, you tell him
what he already knows, he takes it from you, with hands,
you loosen his arm from the shoulder, the right one, the left,
you fasten your arms in their place, with hands, with fingers, with lines,

—what tore off grows back together—
now you have it, now take it, now you have them both,
the name, the name, the hand, the hand,
now take them both as warranty,
he takes that too, and with that you
once more have what is yours, was his,

Windmills

puff air into your lungs, you row
through canals, gullies, lagoons,
by wordlight,
at the stern no Why, at the bow no Whereto, a ram's horn lifts you

—Tekiah!—

wie ein Posaunenschall über die Nächte hinweg in den Tag, die Auguren
zerfleischen einander, der Mensch
hat seinen Frieden, der Gott
hat den seinen, die Liebe
kehrt in die Betten zurück, das Haar
der Frauen wächst wieder,
die nach innen gestülpte
Knospe an ihrer Brust
tritt wieder zutag, lebens-,
herzlinienhin erwacht sie
dir in der Hand, die den Lendenweg hochklomm, —

wie heißt es, dein Land
hinterm Berg, hinterm Jahr?
Ich weiß, wie es heißt.
Wie das Wintermärchen, so heißt es,
en heißt, wie das Sommermärchen,
das Dreijahreland deiner Mutter, das war es,
das ists,
es wandert überallhin, wie die Sprache,
wirf sie weg, wirf sie weg,
dann hast du sie wieder, wie ihn,
den Kieselstein aus
der Mährischen Senke,
den dein Gedanke nach Prag trug,
aufs Grab, auf die Gräber, ins Leben,

längst
ist er fort, wie die Briefe, wie alle
Laternen, wieder
mußt du ihn suchen, da ist er,
klein ist er, weiß,
um die Ecke, da liegt er,

—Tekiah!—
like a trumpet blast out past the nights to the day, the augurs
devour each other, man
has his peace, god
has his, love
returns to the beds, women's
hair grows back,
the involuted bud
on their breast
turns out again, awakens to the life-
heart-lines
in your hand, that climbed up the loinpath—

what is its name, your land
beyond the mountain, the year?
I know its name.
It is named for the Winter's Tale,
for the summer's tale,
the three-year-land of your mother, it was
and is,
it wanders and wanders, like language,
toss it out, toss it out,
then you have it again, as you have it,
the pebble from
the Moravian sink
that bore your thoughts to Prague,
to the grave, on the graves, to life,

it is long
gone, like the letters, like all
the lanterns, again
you must look for it, there
it is, it is little, and white,
around the corner, it lies there,

---

bei Normandie-Njemen—in Böhmen,
da, da, da,
hinterm Haus,
vor dem Haus,
weiß ist er, weiß, er sagt:
Heute—es gilt.
Weiß ist er, weiß, ein Wasser-
strahl findet hindurch, ein Herzstrahl,
ein Fluß,
du kennst seinen Namen, die Ufer
hängen voll Tag, wie der Name,
du tastest ihn ab, mit der Hand:
Alba.

near Normandy—Njemen—in Bohemia,
there, there, there
behind the house,
in front of the house,
it is white, white, it says:
Today—it holds true.
White, it is white, a stream
of water finds its way through, a heartstream,
a river,
you know its name, the banks
hang full of days, like the name,
you feel your way along it, with your hand:
Alba.

IN DEN FLÜSSEN nördlich der Zukunft
werf ich das Netz aus, das du
zögernd beschwerst
mit von Steinen geschriebenen
Schatten.

IN THE RIVERS north of the future
I cast the net, which you
weight hesitantly
with shadows written
by stones.

VOR DEIN SPÄTES GESICHT,
allein-
gängerisch zwischen
auch mich verwandelnden Nächten,
kam etwas zu stehn,
das schon einmal bei uns war, un-
berührt von Gedanken.

BEFORE YOUR LATE FACE
a-
lone between nights
that change me too
something came to stand
that was with us before, once, un-
touched by thoughts.

DIE SCHWERMUTSSCHNELLEN HINDURCH,
am blanken
Wundenspiegel vorbei:
da werden die vierzig
entrindeten Lebensbäume geflößt.

Einzige Gegen-
schwimmerin, du
zählst sie, berührst sie
alle.

DOWN THE RAPIDS OF SADNESS
past the empty
wound mirror:
the forty peeled life trees
are rafted.

Sole anti-
swimmer, you
count them, you touch them
all.

DIE ZAHLEN, im Bund
Mit der Bilder Verhängnis
und Gegen-
verhängnis.

Der drübergestülpte
Schädel, an dessen
schafloser Schläfe ein irr-
lichternder Hammer
all das im Welttakt
besingt.

THE NUMBERS, in league
with the images, with their fateful,
anti-
fatefulness.

The skull clapped over them,
against whose
sleepless temple a will-o'-the-
wispering hammer
sings all that
in worldbeats.

DEIN VOM WACHEN stößiger Traum.
Mit der zwölfmal schrauben-
förmig in sein
Horn gekerbten
Wortspur.

Der letzte Stoß, den er führt.

Die in der senk-
rechten, schmalen
Tagschlucht nach oben
stakende Fähre:
sie setzt
Wundgelesenes über.

YOUR DREAM, wake-prodded,
with the duodenary spiro-
form word-trace
gouged
into its horn.

The final shove that it carries.

In the vertical,
narrow day gorge
the up-tacking
ferry:
it translates
things read raw.

MIT DEN VERFOLGTEN in spätem, un-
verschwiegenem,
strahlendem
Bund.

Das Morgen-Lot, übergoldet,
heftet sich dir an die mit-
schwörende, mit-
schreibende
Ferse.

WITH THE PERSECUTED, in late, un-
concealed
shining
bond.

The morning lead, chased with gold
attached to your con-
spiratorial heel
cursing and writing
along.

WORTAUFSCHÜTTUNG, vulkanisch,
meerüberrauscht.

Oben
der flutende Mob
der Gegengeschöpfe: er
flaggte—Abbild und Nachbild
kreuzen eitel zeithin.

Bis du den Wortmond hinaus-
schleuderst, von dem her
das Wunder Ebbe geschieht
und der herz-
förmige Krater
nackt für die Anfänge zeugt,
die Königs-
geburten.

WORDMOUND, volcanic,
sea-over-rushed.

Above it
the flowing mob
of the anti-creatures: it
signaled—reproduction and copy
tack idly toward time.

Until you fling out the word-
moon, from which
the miracle of ebb occurs
and the heart-
shaped crater,
naked, testifies for the origins,
the kings'
births.

(ICH KENNE DICH, du bist die tief Gebeugte,
ich, der Durchbohrte, bin dir untertan.
Wo flammt ein Wort, das für uns beide zeugte?
Du—ganz, ganz wirklich. Ich—ganz Wahn.)

(I KNOW YOU, you are deeply bowed, are sad,
I do your bidding, am pierced through and through.
What flaming word could witness for us two?
You—who are wholly real. I—wholly mad.)

WEGGEBEIZT vom
Strahlenwind deiner Sprache
das bunte Gerede des An-
erlebten—das hundert-
züngige Mein-
gedicht, das Genicht.

Aus-
gewirbelt,
frei
der Weg durch den menschen-
gestaltigen Schnee,
den Büßerschnee, zu
den gastlichen
Gletscherstuben und -tischen.

Tief
in der Zeitenschrunde,
beim
Wabeneis
wartet, ein Atemkristall,
dein unumstößliches
Zeugnis.

Etched away by your
language's raywind
the variegated talk of what's
merely experienced—
the hundred-tongued lie-
poem, the noem.

Whirled
clear,
free
the way through the human-
shaped snow
the penitents' snow, to the
hospitable
glacier rooms and tables.

Deep
in the times'
cleft
by the honeycomb-ice
awaits, a breathcrystal,
your incontrovertible
witness.

KEINE SANDKUNST MEHR, kein Sandbuch, keine Meister.

Nichts erwürfelt. Wieviel
Stumme?
Siebenzehn.

Deine Frage—deine Antwort.
Dein Gesang, was weiß er?

Tiefimschnee,
　　　　Iefimnee,
　　　　　　　I—i—e.

No more sand art, no sand book, no masters.

Nothing diced for. How many
mute ones?
Seventeen.

Your question—your answer.
Your song, what does it know?

Deepinthesnow
        Intheno,

                I—e—o.

HOHLES LEBENSGEHÖFT. Im Windfang
die leer-
geblasene Lunge
blüht. Eine Handvoll
Schlafkorn
weht aus dem wahr-
gestammelten Mund
hinaus zu den Schnee-
gesprächen.

HOLLOW LIFESTEAD. In the shelter
the blown-
empty lung
blooms. A handful
of sleepseeds
drift from the true-
stammered mouth
out to the snow
conversations.

AM WEISSEN GEBETRIEMEN——der
Herr dieser Stunde
war
ein Wintergeschöpf, ihm
zulieb
geschah, was geschah——
biß sich mein kletternder Mund fest, noch einmal,
als er dich suchte, Rauchspur
du, droben,
in Frauengestalt,
du auf der Reise zu meinen
Feuergedanken im Schwarzkies
jenseits der Spaltworte, durch
die ich dich gehn sah, hoch-
beinig und
den schwerlippigen eignen
Kopf
auf dem von meinen
tödlich genauen
Händen
lebendigen Körper.

Sag deinen dich
bis in die Schluchten hinein-
begleitenden Fingern, wie
ich dich kannte, wie weit
ich dich ins Tiefe stieß, wo
dich mein bitterster Traum
herzher beschlief, im Bett
meines unablösbaren Namens.

ON THE WHITE PHYLACTERY——the
lord of this hour
was
a winter creature, for his
sake
happened, what happened—
my climbing mouth bit itself fast, once again,
as it sought you, smoke trace
you, up there,
in the shape of a woman,
you on the way to my
fiery thoughts, in the pitch
past the split words, through
which I saw you pass, long-
legged,
your own heavy-lipped
head
on the body
alive from my
mortally precise
hands.

Tell your fingers,
that go with you deep
in the cleft, how
I knew you, how far I
thrust you into the deep, where
my bitterest dream mounted you
heartward, in the bed
of my inalienable name.

MITTAGS, bei
Sekundengeflirr,
im Rundgräberschatten, in meinen
gekammerten Schmerz
—mit dir, Herbei-
geschwiegene, lebt ich
zwei Tage in Rom
von Ocker und Rot—:
kommst du, ich liege schon da,
hell durch die Türen geglitten, waagrecht—:

es werden die Arme sichtbar, die dich umschlingen, nur sie. Soviel
Geheimnis
bot ich noch auf, trotz allem.

AFTERNOON, with
whirring seconds,
in the cist tomb shadow, in my
chambered pain
—with you, silenced
over to me, I lived
two days in Rome
on ochre and red—:
you arrive, I am already lying here,
gliding bright through the door, horizontal—:

the arms appear, that embrace you, only they. This much
mystery
I still mustered, in spite of it all.

UNTER DIE HAUT meiner Hände genäht:
dein mit Händen
getrösteter Name.

Wenn ich den Klumpen Luft
knete, unsere Nahrung,
säuert ihn der
Buchstabenschimmer aus
der wahnwitzig-offenen
Pore.

SEWN UNDER THE SKIN of my hands:
your name, comforted
with hands.

When I knead the clump of air,
our nourishment,
its leaven is
the alphabet glimmer from
the absurdly open
pore.

Hafen

Wundgeheilt: wo-,
wenn du wie ich wärst, kreuz-
und quergeträumt von
Schnapsflaschenhälsen am
Hurentisch

—würfel
mein Glück zurecht, Meerhaar,
schaufel die Welle zuhauf, die mich trägt, Schwarzfluch,
brich dir den Weg
durch den heißesten Schoß,
Eiskummerfeder—,

wo-
hin
kämst du nicht mit mir zu liegen, auch
auf die Bänke
bei Mutter Clausen, ja sie
weiß, wie oft ich dir bis
in die Kehle hinaufsang, heidideldu,
wie die heidelbeerblaue
Erle der Heimat mit all ihrem Laub,
heidudeldi,
du, wie die
Astralflöte von
jenseits des Weltgrats—auch da
schwammen wir, Nacktnackte, schwammen,
den Abgrundvers auf
brandroter Stirn—unverglüht grub
sich das tief-
innen flutende Gold
seine Wege nach oben—,

Harbor

Healed raw: where—
if you were like me, dreamed back
and forth by
schnapps bottle necks at the
whores' table

—gamble
my luck straight, ocean hair,
shovel the wave up that carries me, black bane,
break your way
through the hottest of wombs,
ice-heartache feather—

where
then
would you not come to lie with me, even
on the benches
at Mother Clausen's, she
knows how often I sang you right up
to the neck, hey diddle do,
like the blueberry blue
alder of home, with its foliage all,
hey diddle dee,
you, like the
astral flute from
beyond the world's backbone—there too
we swam, bare naked, we swam,
abyssal verses on
fire-red temples—undead ember, the
flowing gold
deeply within, dug
its paths upward—

                    hier,
mit bewimperten Segeln,
fuhr auch Erinnrung vorbei, langsam
sprangen die Brände hinüber, ab-
getrennt, du,
abgetrennt auf
den beiden blau-
schwarzen Gedächtnis-
schuten,
doch angetrieben auch jetzt
vom Tausend-
arm, mit dem ich dich hielt,
kreuzen, an Sternwurf-Kaschemmen vorbei,
unsre immer noch trunknen, trinkenden,
nebenweltlichen Münder—ich nenne nur sie—,

bis drüben am zeitgrünen Uhrturm
die Netz-, die Ziffernhaut lautlos
sich ablöst—ein Wahndock,
schwimmend, davor
abweltweiß die
Buchstaben der
Großkräne einen
Unnamen schreiben, an dem
klettert sie hoch, zum Todessprung, die
Laufkatze Leben,
den
baggern die sinn-
gierigen Sätze nach Mitternacht aus,
nach ihm
wirft die neptunische Sünde ihr korn-
schnapsfarbenes Schleppseil,
zwischen
zwölf-

                              here,
with lashed sails,
memory too floated by, slowly
the flames sprang over, sep-
arated, you,
separated on
the two blue-
black memory
scows
but driven now too
by the thousand-
arm I held you with,
our otherworldly mouths—I name only them—
cross, past the star-cast gin mills,
still drunk, still drinking,

until there by the time-green watchtower
the retina, cipher-skin,
soundlessly pulls out—a mad dock
swimming, in the foreground
unworldly white the
tall crane, its letters
write
a non-name, on it
clambers up, to the salto mortale, the
gantry crane life
to be bulldozed out
past midnight
by sense-hungry sentences,
toward it
the Neptune hour casts its
schnapps-colored tow rope,
between
twelve-

tonigen Liebeslautbojen
—Ziehbrunnenwinde damals, mit dir
singt es im nicht mehr
binnenländischen Chor—
kommen die Leuchtfeuerschiffe getanzt,
weither, aus Odessa,

die Tieflademarke,
die mit uns sinkt, unsrer Last treu,
eulenspiegelt das alles
hinunter, hinauf und—warum nicht? *wundgeheilt, wo-,*

wenn—

herbei und vorbei und herbei.

toned love buoys
—well ropes' winches from once-upon-a-time, with you
it sings in the no longer
landlocked chorus—
the beacon-fire ships come dancing
from far away, from Odessa,

the deep-loading line
that sinks with us, true to our cargo,
it is all Eulenspiegeling
downward, and upward, and—why not? *healed raw, where*—,
                                                    when—
this way, and away, and this way.

EIN DRÖHNEN: es ist
die Wahreit selbst
unter die Menschen
getreten,
mitten ins
Metapherngestöber.

A ROARING: Truth
herself
has gone
among mankind,
straight into the
metaphor flurry.

GROSSE, GLÜHENDE WÖLBUNG
mit dem sich
hinaus- und hinweg-
wühlenden Schwarzgestirn-Schwarm:

der verkieselten Stirn eines Widders
brenn ich dies Bild ein, zwischen
die Hörner, darin,
im Gesang der Windungen, das
Mark der geronnenen
Herzmeere schwillt.

Wo-
gegen
rennt er nicht an?

Die Welt ist fort, ich muß dich tragen.

GREAT, GLOWING MOUND
with the in-and-out
squirming
black-stellar swarm:

On the silicified brow of a ram
I brand this image, between
its horns, in which,
in the song of the windings,
the congealed heart oceans'
marrow swells.

What
does he
not butt against?

The world is gone; I must carry you.

EINMAL,
da hörte ich ihn,
da wusch er die Welt,
ungesehn, nachtlang,
wirklich.

Eins und Unendlich,
vernichtet,
ichten.

Licht war. Rettung.

ONCE
I heard him,
he was washing the world
unseen, night-long,
really.

One and Eternal,
annihilated,
ihilate.

Light was. Salvation.

IN DEN GERÄUSCHEN, wie unser Anfang,
in der Schlucht,
wo du mir zufielst,
zieh ich sie wieder auf, die
Spieldose—du
weißt: die unsichtbare,
die
unhörbare.

IN THE SOUNDS, like our beginning,
in the abyss
where you fell toward me
I wind it up again, the
music box—you
know: the invisible
the
inaudible one.

AUF ÜBERREGNETER FÄHRTE
die kleine Gauklerpredigt der Stille.

Es ist, als könntest du hören,
als liebt ich dich noch.

ON A RAINED-OVER TRACK
the small juggler's sermon of silence.

It is, as if you could hear,
as if I still loved you.

WEISSGERÄUSCHE, gebündelt,
Strahlen-
gänge
über den Tisch
mit der Flaschenpost hin.

(Sie hört sich zu, hört
einem Meer zu, trinkt es
hinzu, entschleiert
die wegschweren
Münder.)

Das Eine Geheimnis
mischt sich für immer ins Wort.
(Wer davon abfällt, rollt
unter den Baum ohne Blatt.)

Alle die
Schattenverschlüsse
an allen den
Schattengelenken,
hörbar-unhörbar,
die sich jetzt melden.

WHITE NOISES, bundled
ray-
focused
across the table, out
with the message in a bottle.

(It listens in to itself, harks
to a sea, drinks it in
too, unveils
the journey-heavy
mouths.)

The One sole secret
mixes in with the word, forever.
(Whoever falls away rolls
under the leafless tree.)

All the
spectral hasps
on all the
spectral joints
audible-inaudible
that announce themselves now.

ENTTEUFELTER NU.
Alle Winde.

Die Gewalten, ernüchtert,
nähn den Lungenstich zu.
Das Blut stürzt in sich zurück.

In Böcklemünd, über die vordere, die
Leichtschrift,
auch über dich,
tieferer Mitbruder Buchstab,
eilt, unendlichkeitsher,
der Hammerglanz hin.

DEDEVILED NOW.
All the winds.

The powers, now sobered,
sew up the punctured lung.
The blood leaps back to itself.

In Böcklemünd, past the initial
light writing
and also past you,
more profound brother letter,
the hammer's polish
scurries off
from eternity.

DU WARST mein Tod:
dich konnte ich halten,
während mir alles entfiel.

YOU WERE my death:
you I could hold
while all escaped me.

DIE ABGEWRACKTEN TABUS,
und die Grenzgängerei zwischen ihnen,
weltennaß, auf
Bedeutungsjagd, auf
Bedeutungs-
flucht.

THE TORN DOWN TABOOS
and the border-crossing between them,
wet with worlds, on the hunt
for meaning,
in flight from
meaning.

STILLE, Fergenvettel, fahr mich durch die Schnellen.
Wimpernfeuer, leucht voraus.

STILLNESS, ferry-bitch, carry me over the rapids.
Lash bonfire, light the way forward.

NAH, IM AORTENBOGEN,
im Hellblut:
das Hellwort.

Mutter Rahel
weint nicht mehr.
Rübergetragen
alles Geweinte.

Still, in den Kranzarterien,
unumschnürt:
Ziw, jenes Licht.

NEAR, IN THE AORTA-ARCH,
in the bright blood:
the bright word.

Mother Rachel
weeps no more.
Carried across
everything wept over.

Still, in the coronary arteries,
unbound:
Ziv, that light.

DENK DIR

Denk dir:
der Moorsoldat von Massada
bringt sich Heimat bei, aufs
unauslöschlichste,
wider
allen Dorn im Draht.

Denk dir:
die Augenlosen ohne Gestalt
führen dich frei durchs Gewühl, du
erstarkst und
erstarkst.

Denk dir: deine
eigene Hand
hat dies wieder
ins Leben
empor-
gelittene
Stück
bewohnbarer Erde
gehalten.

Denk dir:
das kam auf mich zu,
namenwach, handwach
für immer,
vom Unbestattbaren her.

PAUL CELAN

Just Think

Just think:
the *Moorsoldat* of Masada
acquires a homeland, most
unquenchably,
against
each barb in the wire.

Just think:
the eyeless, formless ones
lead you free through the turmoil, you
grow stronger
and stronger.

Just think: your
own hand
held this
clump
of livable earth
suffered
upward
toward life
once again.

Just think:
this came toward me
name-wakened, hand-wakened
forever
from the unburiable.

BEDENKENLOS,
den Vernebelungen zuwider,
glüht sich der hängende Leuchter
nach unten, zu uns

Vielarmiger Brand,
such jetzt sein Eisen, hört,
woher, aus Menschenhautnähe,
ein Zischen,

findet,
verliert,

schroff
liest sich, minutenlang,
die schwere,
schimmernde
Weisung.

WITH NO SECOND THOUGHTS,
against the obscurances,
the menorah glows
downward, to us.

Many-armed blaze
now seeks its iron, hears
from where? a hissing, from the human-skin
closeness,

finds,
loses,

abruptly
for minutes, is read
the weighty,
shimmering
instruction.

NACH DEM LICHTVERZICHT:
der vom Botengang helle,
hallende Tag.

Die blühselige Botschaft,
schriller und schriller,
findet zum blutenden Ohr.

After renouncing light:
bright from the messenger's passage,
the resounding day.

The bloomhappy message,
shriller and shriller,
finds its way to the bleeding ear.

VOM HOCHSEIL herab-
gezwungen, ermißt du,
was zu gewärtigen ist
von soviel Gaben,

Käsig-weißes Gesicht
dessen, der über uns herfällt,

Setz die Leuchtzeiger ein, die Leucht-
ziffern,

Sogleich, nach Menschenart,
mischt sich das Dunkel hinzu,
das du herauserkennst

aus all diesen
unbußfertigen, unbotmäßigen
Spielen.

FROM THE HIGHWIRE, forced
down, you assess
what is to be realized
from so many gifts,

Sheet white face
of the one who falls over us,

Commit the fluorescent hands, the fluorescent
numbers,

At once, in human fashion,
the darkness you recognize
inserts itself

amidst all these
unrepentant, unsuitable
games.

ÜBER DIE KÖPFE
hinweggewuchtet
das Zeichen, traumstark entbrannt
am Ort, den es nannte.

Jetzt:
Mit dem Sandblatt winken,
bis der Himmel
raucht.

OVER THE HEADS
heaved away
the dream-strong sign, inflamed
in the place that it named.

Now:
Wave with the shrub leaf
till the heavens
smoke.

WIRFST DU
den beschrifteten
Ankerstein aus?

Mich hält hier nichts,

nicht die Nacht der Lebendigen,
nicht die Nacht der Unbändigen,
nicht die Nacht der Wendigen,

Komm, wälz mit mir den Türstein
vors Unbezwungene Zelt.

WILL YOU THROW
the lettered
anchorstone out?

Nothing holds me here,

not the night of the living,
not the night of the savage,
not the night of the clever,

Come, let us roll the doorstone
before the unbridled tent.

ANGEFOCHTENER STEIN,
grüngrau, entlassen
ins Enge.

Enthökerte Glutmonde
leuchten
das Kleinstück Welt aus:

das also warst du
auch.

In den Gedächtnislücken
stehn die eigenmächtigen Kerzen
und sprechen Gewalt zu.

Stone, cast into doubt,
greengray, let go
into strictures.

Unhuckstered ember-moons
illumine
that small object world:

so you were that
too.

In the lapses of memory
the high-handed candles stand
urging violence.

EINGEDUNKELT
die Schlüsselgewalt.
Der Stoßzahn regiert,
von der Kreidespur her,
gegen die Welt-
sekunde.

DARKENED IN
the power of the keys.
The tusk is in charge,
from the chalk-trace
against the world-
second.

FÜLL DIE ÖDNIS in die Augensäcke,
den Opferruf, die Salzflut,

komm mit mir zu Atem
und drüber hinaus.

FILL THE WILDERNESS in the eye-bags,
the call to sacrifice, the salt flood.

Come with me to breath
and beyond.

EINBRUCH des Ungeschiedenen
in deine Sprache,
Nachtglast,

Sperrzauber, stärker.

Von fremdem, hohem
Flutgang unterwaschen
dieses
Leben.

INVASION of the unsplit
into your language,
nightglazed,

ban-magic, stronger.

By strange high
floodtide underswept
this
life.

MIT UNS, den
Umhergeworfenen, dennoch
Fahrenden:

der eine
unversehrte,
nicht usurpierbare,
aufständische
Gram.

WITH US, the
buffeted ones, who are yet
underway:

the one
undamaged
non-usurpable
insurgent
grudge.

DIE LEERE MITTE, der wir singen halfen,
als sie nach oben stand, hell,

als sie die Brote vorbeiließ, gesäuert und ungesäuert,

von Rotem umdunkelt, von Andrem,
von Fragen, dir folgend,

seit langem.

THE VACANT CENTER that we helped sing,
when it stood skyward, bright,

when it let the loaves pass, leavened and unleavened,

darkened with redness, with Other,
with questions, following you,

for a long time.

Das am Gluteisen hier

vorbeigedolmetschte Drüben:

So leicht, von Lobgesängen,
wird unsereins nicht satt.

Von sechs Funken her
gesteuerte Härten
kommen. Und kein

Nebenbei.

THE GLOWING BRANDING IRON HERE,
and the There interpreted past it:

So easily, with songs of praise,
such as we are not satisfied.

From six sparks
steered hardnesses come
toward us. And no

by the by.

ERLISCH NICHT GANZ——wie andere es taten
vor dir, vor mir,

das Haus, nach dem Knospenregen,
nach der
Umarmung,
weitet sich über uns aus,
während der Stein
festwächst,

ein Leuchter, groß und allein,
taucht hinzu,
erkennt,
als die Schale, ganz aus Porphyr,
aufbricht, wie
es von Verborgenem
wimmelt, unabwendbar,

erfährt,
wo die offenen Augen jetzt stehn,
morgens, mittags, abends, nachts.

DON'T BE EXTINGUISHED—as others were
before you, before me,

the house, after the budding rain,
after the
embrace,
spreads itself out over us,
while the stone
grows fast,

a menorah, great and alone,
dives to join it
knows
as the vessel, of porphyry,
breaks open, how
it is alive with
things hidden, ineluctably

learns
where the open eyes stand now,
at morning, noontime, evening, night.

WIR LAGEN

schon tief in der Macchia, als du
endlich herankrochst.
Doch konnten wir nicht
hinüberdunkeln zu dir:
es herrschte
Lichtzwang.

WE ALREADY LAY
deep in the maquis, when you
finally crept near.
But we could not
darken over to you:
there was
forced light.

FREIGEGEBEN auch dieser
Start.

Bugradgesang mit
Corona.

Das Dämmerruder spricht an,
deine wach-
gerissene Vene
knotet sich aus,

was du noch bist, legt sich schräg,
du gewinnst
Höhe.

RELEASED, as well, this
take-off.

Song of landing gear with
corona.

The dimmer-switch turns on,
your torn-
awake vein
unknots,

what you still are lies diagonally,
you gain
altitude.

TODTNAUBERG

Arnika, Augentrost, der
Trunk aus dem Brunnen mit dem
Sternwürfel drauf,

in der
Hütte,

die in das Buch
—wessen Namen nahms auf
vor dem meinen?—,
die in dies Buch
geschriebene Zeile von
einer Hoffnung, heute,
auf eines Denkenden
kommendes
Wort
im Herzen,

Waldwasen, uneingeebnet,
Orchis und Orchis, einzeln,

Krudes, später, im Fahren,
deutlich,

der uns fährt, der Mensch,
der's mit anhört,
die halb
beschrittenen Knüppel-
pfade im Hochmoor,

Feuchtes,
viel.

TODTNAUBERG

Arnica, eyebright, the
drink from the well with the
star-die on it

in the
hut,

the lines in the book
—whose name did it welcome
before mine?—
the lines written
in the book
of a hope, today,
of a thinker's
coming
word
in the heart,

forest clearing, rough,
dead man's fingers, single,

crudeness, later, driving,
apparent

the driver, the man
listening in,
the half-
trodden log road
on the high moor

dampness,
much.

EINEM BRUDER IN ASIEN

Die selbstverklärten
Geschütze
fahren gen Himmel,

zehn
Bomber gähnen,

ein Schnellfeuer blüht,
so gewiß wie der Frieden,

eine Handvoll Reis
erstirbt als dein Freund.

To a Brother in Asia

The self-glorified
guns
take aim at heaven,

ten
bombers yawn,

artillery fire blooms,
as surely as peace,

a handful of rice
dies away as your friend.

WIE DU dich ausstirbst in mir:

noch im letzten
zerschlissenen
Knoten Atems
steckst du mit einem
Splitter
Leben.

How YOU die away in me:

even in the last
flayed
knot of breath
you hold on with a
splinter of
life.

SCHWIMMHÄUTE zwischen den Worten,

ihr Zeithof—
ein Tümpel,

Graugrätiges hinter
dem Leuchtschopf
Bedeutung.

WEBS between the swimming words

their temporal corona—
a small pond,

gray fishbones behind
the light bundle
meaning.

ANREDSAM
war die ein-
flüglig schwebende Amsel,
über der Brandmauer, hinter
Paris, droben,
im
Gedicht.

Addressable

was the one-
winged blackbird, hovering
above the burning wall, behind
Paris, up there
in the
poem.

Du sei wie du, immer.

Stant vp Jherosalem inde
erheyff dich

Auch wer das Band zerschnitt zu dir hin,

inde wirt
erluchtet

knüpfte es neu, in der Gehugnis,

Schlammbrocken schluckt ich, im Turm,

Sprache, Finster-Lisene,

קומי
אורי
kumi
ori.

YOU BE LIKE YOU, always.

Stant vp Jherosalem inde
erheyff dich,

even the one who cut the tie to you,

inde wirt
erluchtet,

tied it anew, in the *gehugnis,*

clumps of mud that I gulped, in the tower,

language, dark-faceted.

קומי
אורי
kumi
ori.

DU LIEGST im großen Gelausche,

umbuscht, umflockt.

Geh du zur Spree, geh zur Havel,
geh zu den Fleischerhaken,
zu den roten Äppelstaken
aus Schweden—

Es kommt der Tisch mit den Gaben,
er biegt um ein Eden—

Der Mann ward zum Sieb, die Frau
mußte schwimmen, die Sau,
für sich, für keinen, für jeden—

Der Landwehrkanal wird nicht rauschen.
Nichts
        stockt.

PAUL CELAN

You lie in the great listening,

enbushed, enflaked.

You: go to the Spree, to the Havel,
go to the butchers' hooks,
to the red applesticks
from Sweden—

The table with gifts is coming,
it corners into an Eden—

The man became a sieve, the woman
had to swim, the bitch,
for herself, for no one, for everyone—

The Landwehr Canal won't be rushing.
Nothing
        stops.

UNLESBARKEIT dieser
Welt. Alles doppelt.

Die starken Uhren
geben der Spaltstunde recht,
heiser.

Du, in dein Tiefstes geklemmt,
entsteigst dir
für immer.

ILLEGIBILITY of this
world. Everything double.

The strong clocks
affirm the split-hour,
hoarse.

You, clamped into your deepest place,
climb out of yourself
forever.

ICH HÖRE, DIE AXT HAT GEBLÜHT,
ich höre, der Ort ist nicht nennbar,

ich höre, das Brot, das ihn ansieht,
heilt den Erhängten,
das Brot, das ihm die Frau buk,

ich höre, sie nennen das Leben
die einzige Zuflucht.

PAUL CELAN

I HEAR THAT THE AX HAS BLOSSOMED,
I hear the place cannot be named,

I hear that the loaf that looks at him
heals the hanged man,
the loaf that the women baked for him,

I hear they are calling life
the sole refuge.

DIE NACHZUSTOTTERNDE WELT,

bei der ich zu Gast
gewesen sein werde, ein Name,
herabgeschwitzt von der Mauer,
an der eine Wunde hochleckt.

THE STUTTER-AFTERABLE WORLD,

where I shall have been
a guest, a name
sweated down from the wall
up which a wound licks.

HERVORGEDUNKELT, noch einmal,
kommt deine Rede
zum vorgeschatteten Blatt-Trieb
der Buche.

Es ist
nichts herzumachen von euch,
du trägst eine Fremdheit zu Lehen.

Unendlich
hör ich den Stein in dir stehn.

DARKENED FORTH, once more,
your talk arrives
at the beech tree's fore-shadowed
leafing.

There is
nothing to be made of you all,
alone, you offer up strangeness.

Endlessly, I hear
the stone stand in you.

EIN BLATT, baumlos,
für Bertolt Brecht:

Was sind das für Zeiten,
wo ein Gespräch
beinah ein Verbrechen ist,
weil es soviel Gesagtes
mit einschließt?

A LEAF, treeless,
for Bertolt Brecht:

What times are these
where a conversation
is almost a crime
because it embraces
so much that has been said?

Und Kraft und Schmerz

und was mich stieß
und trieb und hielt:

Hall-Schalt-
Jahre,

Fichtenrausch, einmal,

die wildernde Überzeugung,
daß dies anders zu sagen sei als
so.

AND STRENGTH AND PAIN
and what shoved me
and drove and held:

grace-leap-
years

spruce-drunk, once,

the wilding conviction
that this could be said otherwise than
so.

VON DER SINKENDEN WALSTIRN
les ich dich ab—
du erkennst mich,

der Himmel
stürzt sich
in die Harpune,

sechsbeinig
hockt unser Stern im Schaum,

langsam
hißt einer, der's sieht,
den Trosthappen: das
balzende Nichts.

FROM THE SINKING WHALEBROW
I glean you—
you recognize me,

heaven
casts itself
on the harpoon,

six-legged,
our star squats in the foam,

slowly,
someone watching
hoists the consolation prize: the
cooing void.

ERST WENN ICH DICH
als Schatten berühre,
glaubst du mir meinen
Mund,

der klettert mit Spät-
sinnigem droben
in Zeithöfen
umher,

du stößt zur Heerschar
der Zweitverwerter unter
den Engeln,

Schweigewütiges
sternt.

ONLY WHEN I TOUCH YOU
as shadow
do you believe my
mouth,

which clambers around with things
thought lately, in
temporal coronas, up
there,

you join the army
of re-exploiters among
the angels,

a mad silence
stars.

EINGESCHOSSEN
in die Smaragdbahn,

Larvenschlupf, Sternschlupf, mit allen
Kielen
such ich dich,
Ungrund.

SHOT IN
on the emerald path,

larval moult, star moult, with all
keels
I seek you,
unground.

ALLE DIE SCHLAFGESTALTEN, kristallin,
die du annahmst
im Sprachschatten,

ihnen
führ ich mein Blut zu,

die Bildzeilen, sie
soll ich bergen
in den Schlitzvenen
meiner Erkenntnis—,

meine Trauer, ich seh's,
läuft zu dir über.

ALL THE SLEEP SHAPES, crystalline,
that you assumed
in the shadow of speech,

to them
I deliver my blood,

the image-lines, those
I should recoup
in the slit veins of my
cognition—

my grief, I see it,
slips over to you.

DU WIRFST MIR Ertrinkendem

Gold nach:
vielleicht läßt ein Fisch
sich bestechen.

YOU THROW ME, drowning,

gold:
perhaps a fish
can be bribed.

KLEINE NACHT: wenn du
mich hinnimmst, hinnimmst,
hinauf,
drei Leidzoll überm
Boden:

alle die Sterbemäntel aus Sand,
alle die Helfenichtse,
alles, was da noch
lacht
mit der Zunge—

LITTLE NIGHT: when you
take me to you, take me
up
three agonized inches above
the earth:

all the funereal coats of sand
all the help-me-nots
everything that
still laughs
there
with its tongue—

ICH ALBERE mit meiner Nacht,
wir kapern
alles,
was sich hier losriß,

lad du mir auch deine
Finsternis auf
die halben, fahrenden
Augen,

auch sie soll es hören,
von überallher,
das unwiderlegbare Echo
jeder Verschattung.

I PLAY THE JOKER with my night,
we seize
whatever
was torn loose here,

you: load me up with
your darkness, too,
the half-, the wandering
eyes,

it should hear it, too, from
everywhere, ricocheting—
the irrefutable echo of
every shadowing.

MEINE
dir zugewinkelte Seele
hört dich
gewittern,

in deiner Halsgrube lernt
mein Stern, wie man wegsackt
und wahr wird,

ich fingre ihn wieder heraus—
komm, besprich dich mit ihm,
noch heute.

My
soul, angled toward you,
hears you
thunder,

in the hollow of your neck
my star learns to fall back
and grow true,

I finger it out again—
come, have a talk with it
before day's end.

DIE POSAUNENSTELLE
tief im glühenden
Leertext,
in Fackelhöhe,
im Zeitloch:

hör dich ein
mit dem Mund.

THE TRUMPET PASSAGE
deep in the glowing
vacant text,
at torch height,
in the time-hole:

listen in
with the mouth.

DIE POLE

sind in uns,
unübersteigbar
im Wachen,
wir schlafen hinüber, vors Tor
des Erbarmens,

ich verliere dich an dich, das
ist mein Schneetrost,

sag, daß Jerusalem *ist*,

sags, als wäre ich dieses
dein Weiß,
als wärst du
meins,

als könnten wir ohne uns wir sein,

ich blättre dich auf, für immer,

du betest, du bettest
uns frei.

THE POLES
are in us
insurmountable
waking,
we sleep past them, to the Gate
of Mercy,

I lose you to you, that
is my snow consolation.

Say that Jerusalem is,

say it, as if I were this,
your whiteness,
as if you were
mine,

as if we, without us, could be we,

I leaf you open, forever,

you pray, you bed
us free.

ICH TRINK WEIN aus zwei Gläsern
und zackere an
der Königszäsur
wie Jener
am Pindar,

Gott gibt die Stimmgabel ab
als einer der kleinen
Gerechten,

aus der Lostrommel fällt
unser Deut.

I DRINK WINE from two glasses
and harrow through
the king's caesura
as the other one did
through Pindar,

god strikes the tuning fork
as one of the lesser
righteous ones,

and the drum with the chances decides
our lot.

DAS NICHTS, um unsrer
Namen willen
—sie sammeln uns ein—,
siegelt,

das Ende glaubt uns
den Anfang,

vor den uns
umschweigenden
Meistern,
im Ungeschiednen, bezeugt sich
die klamme
Helle.

THE VOID, for the sake
of our names
—they collect us—
anneals,

the end believes
our beginning,

before the masters
whose silence
surrounds us
in the unsplit, is witnessed
a dank
brightness.

REBLEUTE graben
die dunkelstündige Uhr um,
Tiefe um Tiefe,

du liest,

es fordert
der Unsichtbare den Wind
in die Schranken,

du liest,

die Offenen tragen
den Stein hinterm Aug,
der erkennt dich,
am Sabbath.

VINTNERS harrow
the dark-houred watch, turning
depth over depth

you glean,

the invisible one
orders the wind back
within bounds,

you glean,

the open ones bear
the stone behind the eye,
it knows you,
on the Sabbath.

Notes on the Poems

The following notes are drawn from a variety of sources, including *Paul Celan, Die Gedichte. Kommentierte Gesamtausgabe in einem Band* (ed. with comments by Barbara Wiedemann, Frankfurt am Main: Suhrkamp, 2005—cited as KG); *Paul Celan—Gisèle Celan-Lestrange Briefwechsel* (trans. by Eugen Helmlé, with notes translated by Barbara Wiedemann. Frankfurt am Main: Suhrkamp, 2001—cited as PC-GCL); and John Felstiner, *Paul Celan. Poet. Survivor. Jew* (New Haven and London: Yale University Press, 1995—cited as Felstiner). I have also drawn on Peter Szondi, *Celan Studies*, trans. by Susan Bernofsky with Harvey Mendelsohn (Stanford: Stanford University Press, 2003). *Paul Celan & Ilana Shmueli, Correspondence* (trans. by Susan H. Gillespie. Riverdale-on-Hudson: The Sheep Meadow Press, 2011—cited as PC-IS).

The notes seek to identify proper names or other specific references in the poems. Occasionally they also mention events that occurred immediately prior to the poems' composition. The notes are specifically *not* intended to be interpretive. Readers who know German and are curious to learn more about the background of the poems and other events or readings that may form part of their conscious or unconscious sphere of reference are encouraged to consult the very detailed information that has been collected in the *Kommentierte Gesamtausgabe*. The most important sources remain the poetry and prose of Celan himself.

Corona

A partial lunar eclipse occurred on November 1, 1948. The poem's reference to "the sea in the moon's bloody ray" most likely evokes this event, which is typically accompanied by a reddish light.

On the High Seas

The crest of the city of Paris shows a ship with the motto "fluctuet nec mergitur"— "it floats on the waves but does not sink." (KG 613)

In Memoriam Paul Éluard

This poem was written on the eve of the burial of the poet Paul Éluard. Originally associated with the Surrealists, Éluard later became a committed Communist. He had rejected a call by André Breton to join with other poets and intellectuals in opposing the execution of Zavis Kalandra, a Czech surrealist poet and survivor of the Nazi camps whom the Stalinists condemned as a Trotskyite. Kalandra's death sentence was carried out in 1950. (KG 636-37; Felstiner 66-67)

Shibboleth

According to the Old Testament, the Jews used "shibboleth," a Hebrew word whose first consonant is difficult to pronounce, as a password to detect spies crossing the Jordan River. The "twin red dawn" of the poem references socialist workers' armed resistance against the right-wing seizure of state power in Vienna in 1934, and the resistance of the city of Madrid to Franco's seizure of power in 1936. "No pasarán" (they shall not pass) was the slogan of the International Brigades, which fought in the Spanish Civil War on the side of the Popular Front against the Franco regime. Estremadura, on the Portuguese border, was a stronghold of the Popular Front. (KG 637-38; Felstiner, 81-82)

Tenebrae

Certain prayers that form part of the Christian church services during Holy Week, the period between Christ's death on the cross and his rise from the dead, are called "tenebrae." In a custom reminiscent of Jewish tradition, the tenebrae are accompanied by the extinguishing of candles. The poem also contains echoes of Celan's translation of the film *Night and Fog*, by Alain

---

Resnais, which showed the agony of the gas chambers, and of other books that were beginning to appear describing Hitler's "final solution." Celan translated the text of this film, which was written by Jean Cayrol. (KG 649-50; Felstiner, 101-105 a.o.)

Zurich, "The Stork"

Celan and the poet Nelly Sachs met for the first time in Zurich at the Hotel "Zum Storchen," on an Ascension Day, the Christian holy day celebrating Christ's ascension into heaven forty days after his crucifixion.

Your sudden absence

According to Gisèle Lestrange, Celan's wife, the poem was written after she suffered a fainting spell. Celan had planted beans on the windowsill for their son Eric. (KG 675-76; PC-GCL II 121)

Tübingen, January

Celan had visited the so-called Hölderlin Tower in Tübingen, where the poet Hölderlin, in a state of mental darkness, spent thirty-six years, from 1807 to the end of his life in 1843. He was cared for by a carpenter and his wife. The line "a riddle is the pure in origin"—is taken from Hölderlin's poem "The Rhine." In his correspondence with Ilana Shmueli, Celan explained the background of this poem as follows: "There was ... a word from Hölderlin in one of my poems: 'Tübingen, January.' At the end it says 'Palaksch'; Hölderlin, during his madness, is supposed to have used this word to mean yes and no at the same time." (PC-IS 56)

Ballad of a Vagabond and Swindler

The reference to "Paris emprès Pontoise" links the ballad to François Villon, who used these words in a poem. Sadagora, a village near Celan's birthplace Czernowitz, was a center of Hassidism; the poem may owe its creation in part to a review by an Austrian writer who had mentioned "Hassidic traits"

---

in Celan's poetry—a comment Celan found offensive. Heine's poem "To Edom" (contained in a letter to his friend Moses Moser and published only posthumously) refers to a tribe that was hostile to the tribes of Israel; the poem is directed against Jew-haters in general. The quote, "*Friuli./* There we would have…" is borrowed from a sixteenth century ditty sung by mercenary soldiers, who often participated in pogroms (the phrase continued "…would have had a mouthful"). "The Juniper Tree" is a short story by the Brothers Grimm in which a mother who has murdered her children serves them up, as a stew, to their father as he sits under a juniper tree. The pest was frequently given as an excuse for pogroms. (KG 682-85)

In One

February 13, 1962, was the date of a million-strong demonstration in Paris protesting the murder of eight peaceful demonstrators against the war in Algeria and the OAS *(Organisation de l'armée secrète)*. Abadias, the "old man from Huesca," was a former shepherd who had fled to Normandy as a refugee from the Spanish civil war. The battleship Aurora fired on the Hermitage (the palace of the Czar in St. Petersburg) in 1917 to launch the Russian Revolution. Toscana is a reference to Russian poet Osip Mandelstam, whom Celan translated and whose poems, Celan told Ilana Shmueli, were "closest to me among the translations." Mandelstam, who was sent by Stalin to the Gulag, where he died, is said to have recited poems by the Tuscany-born Petrarch in an attempt to save his life. "Peace to the huts," a slogan borrowed from the French revolution, was used by German Poet Georg Büchner in a revolutionary tract called the *Hessian Courier* (*Der Hessische Landbote*). Celan was intensively engaged with Büchner's writing as he prepared the "Meridian" speech he gave in 1960 on being awarded the Georg Büchner Prize, Germany's highest literary honor. (KG 637-38)

Crowned out

Berenice's Hair (Latin: *coma Berenices*) is a constellation named for the Egyptian queen Berenice II, who in the third century B.C.E. sacrificed her blonde hair to assure her husband Ptolomy III victory in battle. On Petrarch, see

---

the note to "In One," above, with its link to Osip Mandelstam. The "Varsovienne," a Polish revolutionary song, also links to Mandelstam, who was born in Warsaw. (KG 702)

La Contrescarpe

Place de la Contrescarpe is a square in Paris that Celan frequented; among other things it is known for the presence of many homeless people. On his way to study medicine in Tours, France, Celan's train passed through Berlin's Anhalter Station on November 8, 1938, one night before the violent attacks on Jews that occurred throughout Germany and Austria on November 9-10 and are known as *Kristallnacht,* or the "Night of Broken Glass." Celan's second trip to France, when he left Vienna in 1948 to take up residence in the French capital, brought him to Paris on July 14, Bastille Day, which celebrates the storming of the Bastille Prison in 1789 during the French Revolution. (KG 710-11)

Everything is otherwise

Karelia is a region of Russia, north of St. Petersburg. The reference to the "bow" of a boat—*Bug* in German—also names the River Bug, where the concentration camp Michaelovka was located, and where Celan's father and mother both died, his father of disease, his mother by gunshot. *Tekiah* (Hebrew) refers to the sound of the shofar, or ram's horn, as it is traditionally sounded on Rosh Hashanah and Yom Kippur. Jewish-German poet Heinrich Heine is the author of the long poem "Germany. A Winter's Tale" *(Deutschland. Ein Wintermärchen).* Celan's mother spent three years as a refugee in Bohemia (within the Moravian sink, or lowland). Njemen, in Normandy, was the home town of a famous French fighter squadron that, during World War II, helped defeat the Nazis in the decisive battle of Stalingrad. Alba, the feminine form of the adjective *albus* ("white"), is also the Latin name of the River Elbe. (KG 711-13)

Down the rapids of sadness

In Celan's fortieth year he received the Büchner Prize. It was also the year in which the infamous campaign by Claire Goll, who accused Celan of plagiarizing her husband Ivan Goll's work, reached its high point (or low point).

Dedeviled Now

This is the first published poem written by Celan following an attempt to commit suicide by stabbing himself in the chest. The knife missed the heart and entered his lung. Celan was confined to a hospital and then a mental ward; he remained an ambulatory patient for several additional months, with permission to leave the hospital. Böcklemünd is the name of the Cologne neighborhood where the city's Jewish cemetery is located. Celan had recently visited the grave of a friend from his youth who had died in an accident. (KG 767)

You were

On the day he wrote this poem, Celan had received a letter from his wife, Gisèle Lestrange, asking for a separation, on the grounds that she feared having a nervous breakdown. (KG 768)

Just Think

The poem "Just Think" was written during and immediately following the 1967 Six-Days War between Israel and its Arab neighbors, in which Israel was victorious. *Moorsoldat* means "peat bog soldier." It is the title of a song written by political prisoners in the concentration camp Börgermoor. A version by Kurt Weill was made famous in the U.S. by Paul Robeson. The city of Masada was the last holdout of Jewish fighters who resisted an attack by Roman soldiers in the year 73 C.E. According to legend, the Jews committed suicide rather than suffer defeat and captivity. (KG 790-91)

With no second thoughts

The poem was written during Passover week. (KG 792)

Over the heads

The shrub leaf is the leaf of the tobacco plant nearest to the stalk. It is considered particularly good for making cigars.

The vacant center

Written during Passover week 1966. (KG 943)

Todtnauberg

Celan met with Martin Heidegger on July 25, 1967, at the philosopher's famous hut in the Black Forest village of Todtnauberg, near Freiburg. During their conversation, Celan asked Heidegger to make a public statement that would clearly disassociate him from his past involvement with the Nazis. Celan believed that he had received an encouraging answer, but Heidegger never did make such a statement, despite the fact that Celan had a presentation copy of the poem "Todtnauberg" specially printed and sent to him. Shortly before his suicide in 1970, Celan gave a reading in Freiburg that was attended by Heidegger. Celan felt that the philosopher did not understand his poems. See: Lyon, James K., *Paul Celan & Martin Heidegger. An Unresolved Conversation, 1951-1970* (Baltimore: The Johns Hopkins University Press, 2006).

You be like you

Celan cites a sermon by medieval mystic Meister Eckhardt, who spoke of powers of the soul, including *gehugnis*, or memory. The Hebrew characters that are spoken as "kumi ori" mean "Arise, shine," and are drawn from the Bible, Isaiah 60.1. (KG 828-29)

You lie in the great listening

Celan wrote this poem during a wintry trip to Berlin in 1967, where he visited the site of the murder of Rosa Luxemburg and Karl Liebknecht. The murderers, acting on orders of the Social Democratic Party, which had just carried out a—briefly—successful coup d'état, were quartered in the Hotel Eden and brought the two Spartacus League members there after their arrest. Liebknecht was shot multiple times; Luxemburg was also shot and her body thrown into the nearby Landwehr Canal. Peter Szondi, who was with Celan in Berlin, wrote extensively about this poem in his *Celan Studies*, emphasizing both the factual background of the poem and its deeper meanings. Szondi's book is available in English in the translation of Susan Bernofsky with Harvey Mendelsohn (Stanford: Stanford University Press, 2003). (KG 832-33)

Darkened forth, once more

This is one of the poems Celan sent to Ilana Shmueli, the friend of his youth whom he fell in love with during the last year of his life. The beech tree, German "Buche," is encoded in Bukovina, the province where their home city of Czernowitz is located.

A tree, leafless

Berthold Brecht had famously asked, rhetorically, "What times are these, when a conversation about trees is almost a crime?"

The poles

The Gate of Mercy, also known as the Golden Gate, is one of the twelve gates to the city of Jerusalem. It is located on the eastern side of the city and bricked shut. According to legend, it will open to receive the Messiah when he returns.

I drink wine

"The other one" refers to Friedrich Hölderlin, whose translations of Pindar were long considered to be incomprehensible. (PS-IS 56)

Index of Titles and First Lines (German)

Index of Titles and First Lines (English)

Water, Light, Darkness, Stone
In the Space of Translation with Paul Celan

> The poem is an occurrence of itself.
> —Paul Celan

The poem is an event
a slice of life
a sluice
luce = light

there was something here that I wanted to capture
that eluded me.

The way light slices through water
the water always moving
the way we want to capture the moving water in the moving light
with a net that is always moving
but our net, the net of our thought, is not light, is
gray, a veil that is always
moving
is dark, or
silvered,
a spider's web in the dew
that tender
and easily torn.

The way thought moves down a nerve
in the form
of a wave
energetically and slowly, at one to thirty meters per second
an oscillation, until it meets itself again, between
hippocampus and prefrontal cortex,

as slowly
as memory, as the chiming of time
in tune with itself
more precisely: of something
in tune with itself
the slight, the ever-so-slight
temporal gap, the same difference that makes time
chime
in the mind
only there
only once
its unseen
eddy
a singularity
once
then again—

The poem:
its moving net of light not merely light but
event potentials' semi-permanent
dynamic state
still, semi is something
between is and as
between is and was
is and was not.

The poem:
the overlapping of references
the phenomenon of interference
the impact of coherent waves on each other when they meet.[1]

---

[1] Text in italics is Paul Celan's.

You have been there before
you have been here before

> *Where was it going? Toward still resounding.*
> *With the stone, went with us twain.*

The wellspring rushes
the endless pool
black ponds of bliss
called by the sea
a river
of darkness
sea–over–rushed
in the deep sea of a soul
and all the seas came too.

And in my eyes there is that moveable veil
it plays
to the tune of that rushing,
images and gestures, veiled and unveiled
as in a dream
the net of light
plays over the stones,
while the stone grows fast
so clear
so perfectly
surreal
more real than real
above real, and below
and over the water a word
that lays the ring over the stone.

> *You opened your eyes—I see my darkness live.*
> *I see down to the bottom;*
> *there too it's mine and lives.*

Can this cross over? And thereby awaken?
Whose light follows at my heels
that a ferryman appeared?

The poem:
with its human freight
a hope, today, of a thinker's human word
in the heart——

borne over water
the sound of words
their coronas
(corona: the halo, the
visual, temporal aura
surrounding
our words)
their likeness
in darkness:
a known-unknown
voice
hear (here)
in the rushing of thought
in your ears
my ears
the ears of our mind.

From darkness to darkness
by strange high floodtide
underswept,
this life.

Listen in
with the mouth
said Celan,

listen in
with the eyes
the eyes on your chest.

You know of the stones
you know of the waters.

Listen in.

Sources in Paul Celan's Writing

꜡

the overlapping of references
the phenomenon of interference
the impact of coherent waves on each other when they meet
                —Conversation with Hugo Huppert, December 26, 1966
(my translation), taken from "'Spirituell.' Ein Gespräch mit Paul Celan."
In: *Paul Celan,* ed. Werner Hamacher and Winfried Menninghaus.
                Frankfurt am Main: Suhrkamp, 1988, 319–24.

Where was it going? Toward still resounding.
With the stone, went with us twain

                                        —"What occurred?"

the wellspring rushes

                                        —"Crystal"

the endless pool

                                        —"Glimmer Tree"

black ponds of bliss

                                        —"Landscape"

called by the sea

                                        —"Still Life"

sea-over-rushed

                                        —"Wordmound"

in the deep sea of a soul
—"Edgar Jené and the Dream about the Dream,"
In *Paul Celan: Collected Prose*,
trans. by Rosmarie Waldrop (Exeter: Carcanet, 1986).

and all the seas came too
—"There was earth in them"

and in my eyes there is that moveable veil
—"Conversation in the Mountains," in *Paul Celan: Collected Prose*.

images and gestures, veiled and unveiled
as in a dream
—"Edgar Jené and the Dream about the Dream"

while the stone grows fast
—"Don't be extinguished"

and over the water a word
that lays the ring over the stone
—"I heard someone say"

You opened your eyes—I see my darkness live.
I see down to the bottom;
there too it's mine and lives.

Can this cross over? And thereby awaken?
Whose light follows at my heels
that a ferryman appeared?
—"From Darkness to Darkness"

a hope, today, of a thinker's human word
in the heart

—"Todtnauberg"

by strange, high floodtide
underswept,
this life

—"Invasion"

listen in
with the mouth

—"The Trumpet Passage"

the eyes ... on your chest

—"Edgar Jené and the Dream about the Dream"

you know of the stones
you know of the waters

—"Shibboleth"

ABOUT THE TRANSLATOR

PHOTO: SUSAN QUASHA

SUSAN H. GILLESPIE has translated works by Theodor W. Adorno and other writers of musicological and philosophical works, as well as fiction and poetry. Her involvement with German and commitment to the idea and practice of translatability go back to five and a half years spent as a student in Freiburg im Breisgau, with the support of the German Academic Exchange Office (DAAD), and a subsequent year in Berlin. She has worked in factories, offices, non-profit institutions, and since 1985 as vice president of Bard College. At Bard, she founded the Institute for International Liberal Education, helping to develop and administer dual degree and academic exchange programs with university partners in Russia, South Africa, Palestine, and Germany, among other places.

Her translation of *The Correspondence of Paul Celan & Ilana Shmueli* (Sheep Meadow Press) was a finalist for the National Translation Award.